The Persistence of Poverty

The Persistence of Poverty

Why the Economics of the Well-off Can't Help the Poor

Charles Karelis

Yale University Press   New Haven and London

Set in Galliard type by Keystone Typesetting, Inc.
Printed in the United States of America by Edwards Brothers, Inc.

Library of Congress Cataloging-in-Publication Data
Karelis, Charles.
The persistence of poverty : why the economics of the well-off can't help the poor /
Charles Karelis.
p. cm.
Includes bibliographical references and index.
ISBN 978-0-300-12090-7 (alk. paper)
1. Poverty — Psychological aspects. 2. Marginal utility. I. Title.
HC79.P6K37 2007
339.4'6 — dc22   2006102206

A catalogue record for this book is available from the British Library.

The paper in this book meets the guidelines for permanence and durability of the Commit-
tee on Production Guidelines for Book Longevity of the Council on Library Resources.

10 9 8 7 6 5 4 3 2 1

I would like to dedicate this book to the memory of my father.

Contents

Preface

The idea that poverty is persistent is, itself, persistent. In its earliest versions, the idea was that poverty is part of the natural order. The book of Deuteronomy says, "The poor shall never cease from the land." Jesus echoes this when he says, shortly before his death, "For the poor you will have with you always, but you do not always have me." Modern writers, too, see poverty as persistent, but not as natural. It strikes them instead as a puzzling anomaly, since now there is enough wealth to go around. Henry George, the most popular American economist of the nineteenth century, entitled a book chapter "The Persistence of Poverty Amid Wealth." Contemporary American writers regularly take society to task over the fact that the U.S. poverty rate has been essentially the same for forty years, despite significant increases in the per capita domestic product.

But if the persistence of poverty is an enduring idea, it is not necessarily a clear one. Logically speaking, the phenomenon of poverty could persist even if no individual was poor for very long. The ranks of "the poor" could be filled by a succession of different people experiencing brief episodes of need. And yet granted that poverty could be persistent on the social level and not the individual level, poverty is actually persistent on both levels. Regarding people born poor, for example, rags to riches makes a good story, but rags to rags isn't news. It's too common. For the case of the United States, this can be confirmed statistically. Relevant data have been compiled by the economist Thomas Hertz and published in *Unequal Chances: Family Background and Economic Success,* edited by Samuel Bowles, Herbert Gintis, and Melissa Osborne Groves (Princeton and Oxford, 2005). These data show that children born in the lowest 10 percent of families ranked by income have a 51 percent probability of ending up in the lowest 20 percent as adults. Roughly speaking, this means that people born very poor face a greater than even chance of ending up moderately or very poor. More striking still, African Americans born very poor have a greater than 40 percent chance of being not just moderately poor but very poor as adults.

The focus of this book is the persistence of poverty in this individual sense. Why do poor people often stay poor? Among the most important causes are five behaviors or, better, nonbehaviors: not working, not finishing school, not saving for a rainy day, not moderating alcohol consumption, and not living within the law. Obviously not all poor people fail to do these things. But poor people fail to do them disproportionately. They account for more than their share of nonworkers, non–school finishers, and so on. And this contributes to their poverty.

But this just pushes the question of causation back. Why do poor people fail to do these things to begin with? Isn't this, too, like poverty amid wealth, a puzzling anomaly? At first glance it seems positively irrational of poor people not to work, not to finish school, and not to moderate alcohol consumption — since the latter interferes with earning. After all, poor people need money the most. And at first glance it seems irrational for anyone, rich or poor, not to save and not to live within the law. For a dollar means more to someone when he has fewer dollars than when he has more. So people who smooth consumption over time, transferring dollars from their relatively rich time-slices to their relatively poor ones, wring more benefit from their resources than people who let their consumption vary by failing to save and pursuing risky careers.

Here, then, is the puzzle. Are poor people really thwarting their own interests, as they seem to be? Many of the theories of poverty that are debated every day in classrooms, in the newspapers, and around watercoolers are responses to this puzzle. Three of the most familiar theories grant that the irrational-looking behavior is in fact irrational and trace it to psychological dysfunctions. One of these three finds the roots of the behavior in poor people's apathy, another in their limited time horizons, and the third in their weakness of will. By contrast three further theories try to show that the behavior is rational after all, the first by reference to opportunity constraints, the second by citing atypical preferences, and the third by invoking perverse incentives created by public policy.

I want to persuade you that the appeal of all six of these theories leans heavily on a mistake. Following a century-old orthodoxy of economics, which has crept from textbooks into common sense, the main accounts of poverty start by misidentifying the kinds of allocations that draw the most benefit from truly scarce resources. So the conventional poverty debate gets off on the wrong foot. It can hardly matter whether the poverty-causing behaviors *truly* fail the textbook test of economic rationality—which is the starting point of dysfunctionalism—or only *seem* to fail it—as the conventional rationalizers contend—if the textbook test of rationality is not the true test. When economic rationality is understood properly, the poverty-linked conduct emerges as being (in general) straightforwardly rational. It is rational, that is, even if we do not assume that it is shaped by restricted opportunities, atypical preferences, or counterproductive public policies. Or so I will argue.

Generally speaking, then, it is the very rationality of the poverty-causing behaviors that explains their persistence—and hence the persistence of individual poverty itself. In that sense, poverty is a self-sustaining condition, not a self-eliminating one. Here is the grain of truth in the ancient idea that poverty is natural. Neither interventions to improve psychological function nor the elimination of conduct-distorting environmental factors will make a great difference to the number of poor people who work, finish school, save, and so on.

This may seem to be a counsel of despair or at least of pessimism. But it is not. Natural does not mean ineradicable. There is a constructive option, and that is to make the poverty-reducing behaviors rational instead of irrational for the people who are poor. But how? What should we do differently to help if we believe the theory? Because I know most about the United States, I raise this question in the American context, but I suspect the issues are similar in many countries. In particular, I look back at the debate surrounding the 1996 U.S. welfare reform, concluding that the policy choice between preserving work incentives and guaranteeing income, however agonizing, is not a choice that had to be made. For no-strings welfare of the old type had a positive effect on work incentives, contrary to the nearly universal consensus of policymakers. In light of this, I raise the possibility that no-strings assistance should remain in the antipoverty policy arsenal, while granting that this is politically improbable. As for currently popular policies designed to encourage work by "making work pay," I view them favorably, indeed, more favorably than they are viewed by conventional economics. I also examine the implications of my theory for the other poverty-causing behaviors. What strategies might be more effective in promoting school persistence, saving, and obeying the law?

Finally, some cautions to readers. This book is meant for both generalists and specialists, and that has entailed a bit of inefficiency. To avoid sending general readers to other sources or asking them to take too much on trust, I have included material that will already be familiar to poverty specialists. For instance, specialists will find nothing new in the survey in chapter 2 of statistical evidence that nonwork, early school leaving, nonsaving, immoderate drinking, and crime occur disproportionately among the poor and contribute to their poverty. (On the other side, some general readers may decide to hurry through chapter 2 on the ground that these claims are too obvious to need statistical support!) Economists will learn no economics from chapter 4, which explains marginalism and the rule of equimarginal allocation. But they may wish to skim chapter 4 anyway for its sketch of how these ideas evolved, because I use this history later, in chapter 6, to account for the virtually universal acceptance of marginalism — despite its being incorrect. Finally, chapter 8 applies the main ideas of the book to a new topic, which will interest some readers more than others. Rather than pursuing the question, What are the causes and cures of poverty? chapter 8 asks a version of the normative question, What is economic justice? How should societies balance respect for market-determined allocation with the principle of allocating goods according to need? The interest of this chapter may be further limited by the fact that my reasoning presupposes the utilitarian goal of making the collective well-being the greatest it can be, which not everyone accepts as the highest moral principle.

Yet another caution is that the book does not deal with poverty so severe that getting food and other resources is an immediate matter of life and death. For instance, it does not deal with the plight of famine victims in sub-Saharan Africa, who are literally dying of hunger. I believe that the motivations of these people are different in kind and not only in degree from those of people whose poverty is less extreme. Something like a survival instinct affects the actions of those who are barely keeping their heads above water, even if its operation is often undermined by physical weakness and disease. Therefore the utility function for insufficient but above survival-level consumption that I give in chapters 5 and 6 may not be suitable for extrapolation to those who are just barely clinging to life. Perhaps the function is discontinuous as consumption crosses the threshold of literal survival. I am sorry to say that I do not have a clear view on this question, and so my hypothesis should be understood as applying only to above survival-level consumption.

Acknowledgments

I would like to thank the following people for insightful comments, in many cases extensive, about ideas in this book and the way I have presented them. No one has been more helpful all along the way than Gordon Winston of the Williams College Department of Economics. Gordon is an exceptionally smart, judicious, and generous colleague. Also, from that department during the period when I first worked on these issues, I would gratefully acknowledge Henry Bruton, Roger Bolton, Ralph Bradburd, Michael McPherson, David Ross, Morton Schapiro, Dana Stevens, and the late Richard Sabot. I would also like to thank the Williams philosophers Dan O'Connor, Alan White, and Will Dudley as well as Mark Taylor from the Department of Religion. My philosophy colleagues at Colgate University Maudmarie Clark, Jon Jacobs, David McCabe, and Ed Witherspoon provided important feedback, as have my philosophy colleagues at The George Washington University: Peter Caws, David DeGrazia, Paul Churchill, Gail

Weiss, Michelle Friend, Eric Saidel, and Jeff Brand-Ballard. From the George Washington University Law School, Fred Lawrence, Ira Lupu, Tom Morgan, John Duffy, and Michael Abramowicz gave me useful comments. From Yale Law School, Anne Alstott and Richard Brooks reacted with great insight to a version of chapter 5. Other assistance was supplied through correspondence with Daniel Hausman, Hal Varian, David Friedman, and James Griffin. Ronald Dworkin, Paul Kelleher, and Alan Ryan were good enough to consider my ideas in conversation. Joan Straumanis was generous with her time and wisdom and saved me from numerous mistakes, as did Arthur McKee of the Citybridge Foundation. Carol Graham of the Brookings Institution and Helen Ladd of the public policy school of Duke University both commented very helpfully from the economist's standpoint on parts of the manuscript, as did Tom Kane, Charles Taylor, and Jim Smith. Robert Goldfarb of the George Washington Economics Department was kind enough to review the graphical analysis in the appendix to chapter 5. Anthony Kronman of Yale Law School gave me detailed comments, good counsel, and opportunities for which I am deeply grateful. I am also very indebted to Johanna Halford Macleod for her unflagging support of this project over the lengthy course of its evolution. My sons, Alex and Oliver, have been tough but fair critics. Alex has helped me see many everyday applications of the theory, and Oliver's account of his year in Micronesia was crucial to chapter 1. Bob Weinberger helped keep me from overlooking recent developments in policy and behavioral economics, and Fred Kellogg shared his good political judgment as I wrote chapter 7. My good friend Austin Frum brought to my attention the adage Comfort the afflicted and afflict the comfortable, which so well summarizes the book. The George Washington University provided me with a stimulating environment in which to write and some extra time off from teaching, and I owe enormous thanks to Steve Trachtenberg and Don Lehman for that. My research assistant Ann Church did a good job critiquing drafts and digging up information. My research assistant Elizabeth Ramey also found lots of data and gave me useful, substantive feedback, and she worked tirelessly with me on the final preparation of the manuscript. Finally, my wife, Heidi Hatfield, has provided wonderful personal support and encouragement, and I am especially grateful to her.

What Poverty Is

Nobody with a practical interest in poverty can be overjoyed to spend time defining it. Semantic issues look like a distraction from the serious business of helping the poor. But those who seek the causes and cures of poverty can easily find themselves in spurious disagreement (or spurious agreement) if they do not first make clear what it is they are talking about.

Two Ways to Define Poverty

Frustratingly, there is a hard choice to be made before one can begin defining poverty. Should the definition be descriptive or stipulative? One approach seems to risk vagueness and ambiguity, while the other seems to risk irrelevance. For in ordinary usage "poverty" has a fuzzy boundary, like the line between red and orange. Who can say at what consumption level being poor ends and being nonpoor begins, even within a given country? What is more, "poverty" appears to mean different things in different parts of the world. Poverty in the United States includes conditions that would not count as poverty in Central Europe, and poverty in Central Europe includes conditions that would not count as poverty in sub-Saharan Africa. This makes it tempting to stipulate a definition. Why not just pick one of the meanings of this spongy word and tell the reader that for the sake of reaching definite conclusions I will use the word "poverty" to mean such-and-such a level of consumption?

But if stipulating avoids vagueness and ambiguity, it risks irrelevance. For by bringing in a special meaning for the key term "poverty," one takes a chance that one may be answering questions that nobody — at least nobody outside the research and policy community — is asking when they ask about poverty.

In this book I am going to take my chances with the first horn of the dilemma in order to make sure I avoid irrelevance. I propose to define "poverty" in the ordinary sense of the word rather than stipulate a new sense. This seems better for two reasons. First, "poverty" in the ordinary sense is (as we will see) neither as vague nor as ambiguous as it appears. Second, the whole investigation is likelier to be of general interest.

The Ordinary Meaning of "Poverty"

The Oxford English Dictionary defines "poverty" as "indigence," and it defines "indigent" as "lacking in what is requisite." Greg J. Duncan concurs: "Poverty has been defined as a state in which resources are insufficient to meet basic needs."[1] The two definitions are close, but Duncan's amendments are significant. First, the unmet needs constituting poverty are needs for "resources," presumably money or the things it can buy. Second, the unmet needs that make someone poor are "basic" needs — requirements one cannot fail to have, regardless of one's particular purposes.

But this just pushes the definition problem back a step. Now we need to ask which needs are basic. Seeing that we are all physical creatures, basic needs must include physical needs like the need for food. But the needs that matter in deciding whether someone is poor must also include any *nonphysical* needs that are universal. For example, the needs for dignity, self-respect, and social inclusion are widely seen as universal, even though not directly tied to physiology. Poverty, then, is essentially a lack of physical resources, but it is not necessarily a matter of unmet physical needs. Rather, poverty is having insufficient material resources to meet all basic needs, whether these basic needs stem from our animal nature or not.

Some Things Poverty Is Not: Having Unfulfilled Wants, Having Very Little, and Having Less Than Others

If being poor is not having what one needs, it is not just a matter of not having what one *wants*. This makes sense because not having everything one wants is a nearly universal condition, after all, while poverty is not. Another implication is that poverty is not a matter of having very little money — or having very little of what money can buy. True, many poor people do have very little, and many people who have very little are poor. But the two things are distinct. If a population's needs are few, they may be able to meet their needs and not be poor, despite a lack of material things. On most of the islands of the Chuuk state, in Micronesia, there are no cars, telephones, clinics, or running water and no regular supply of electricity for domestic use. But the inhabitants are not poor, and this is confirmed by the fact that the English speakers among them do not describe themselves this way. They are not poor because they do not lack what their society recognizes as the requisites of life. It is true that many of the young people of Chuuk envy the living standards of the industrial nations. But they recognize the difference between wanting and needing.[2] Conversely, a natural disaster that somehow annihilated a quarter of the wealth of the United States would leave it with a great deal of wealth, but given the habits of the people it would doubtless be seen as having impoverished the nation.

Another implication of the definition is that being poor is not strictly a matter of having less than others. Studies show that poverty and having less than others are highly correlated, in fact, because people generally feel a need to participate in their society, and this is a need that cannot be easily satisfied at resource levels far below the median. But the idea of poverty is nevertheless distinct from that of having less than others. For one thing, in a nation suffering from famine, even people with more than others — not less — may nevertheless be starving and desperately poor. Conversely, someone might have less than others and not be poor. For grant that there is a universal need for social inclusion, and grant that having much less than others gets in the way of this. Still, relative resource levels could in principle be decoupled from dignity, self-respect, social inclusion, and any other of the nonphysical needs that supposedly have to be fulfilled to avoid poverty. Mickey Kaus recommends that Americans should accord the status of full and respected participant in society to everyone, regardless of their income. If this were to happen, then having less than others would not in fact spell exclusion or therefore poverty, if in fact one's other basic needs were met.[3]

Poverty and Misery

The essence of poverty is lacking the material resources to meet basic needs. But if so, then poverty is bound to be a source of unhappiness. Indeed, that is putting it mildly. Having less than one *needs* means being threatened with diminishment or even extinction. Does that entail that poor people are unhappy *on balance?* Common observation shows that being miserable with respect to one's consumption does usually mean being miserable on balance. Having more material goods than one needs may not guarantee happiness, but having less largely guarantees unhappiness.

Against the idea that poverty means misery it might be argued that some of the best things in life are free, and if social inclusion could be detached from income, à la Kaus, more of the best things in life could be made free. Maybe poor people could be happy on balance after all. But in the world as we find it, satisfactions that come from nonmaterial goods rarely do more than *mitigate* the misery of material shortages. Can even the greatest philosophy make an ill-fed, ill-clothed, and ill-housed person happy overall? One person who thought the misery of material deficits could be outweighed by the consolations of philosophy was Plato. He has Socrates insist in *The Republic* that the wise man in prison is happier than the unwise man outside it, but philosophy would be a much more popular pursuit than it is if Plato had been correct. More cynically, Karl Marx said that religion was the opiate of the masses, meaning the materially poor. But it would be truer to say that religion has sometimes been the weak analgesic of the masses. For opiates kill pain and produce pleasure, while religion mainly consoles. In short, the dictionary definition of poverty, together with the weakness of nonphysical compensations, implies that to be poor is usually to be miserable, period. This is an important result because being miserable on balance imposes a much stronger obligation on others to help than being miserable in this or that particular respect.

Now, not everyone agrees that poor people are typically miserable. One dissenter is Charles Murray, who presents a set of thought experiments designed to show that a Westerner could assimilate into a near-subsistence peasant society, becoming typical in many ways, and yet be quite happy.[4] For instance, he imagines himself becoming a happy rice farmer in Thailand, with a Thai peasant wife, and so on. But Murray's thought experiments do not support his conclusion. He does not succeed in showing that someone can be (a) poor, (b) typical, and (c) happy, because he has not imagined himself poor in the first place. He has imagined himself as having a small income, which is another matter. As we have shown, it is having unmet resource needs, not having few resources, that constitutes poverty. While a typical person can doubtless be happy with few material resources in some societies, that is irrelevant to the question whether a typical person can be happy though poor. Given the meaning of the word "poverty," that is impossible.

Varying Conceptions of Basic Need

So far, so good. But before one can say that the concept of poverty has been made clear enough, there is another issue to be tackled. What gets called a basic need depends on who is making the call. There are many kinds of variation to consider. Individuals living in the same time and place often consider different needs basic. What are typically judged to be requisites in a given society at one time have often been seen as frills at an earlier, less prosperous time in the same society. What are typically judged to be basic needs in one society at a given time may be typically seen as frills in another, contemporary society. And so on. The question is, Is poverty itself something different, depending on these different conceptions of basic needs?

Within a Given Society Varying Conceptions of Basic Need Have Little Impact on What Counts as Poverty

The case of varying views of need in the same society is the simplest. There does seem to be a bit of variation within a given society in what counts as being poor, depending on variations in the level of consumption where people begin to feel the pinch. It makes some sense to say that Smith is poor at a certain level of resources, though his neighbor Jones would not be poor at that same level of resources, if Smith and Jones have different needs. But the concept of poverty is such that any variation in the poverty thresholds between individuals in the same society is bound to be small, even if the variation in their pain thresholds is great. That is because, as others have noted, judgments of poverty put a lot of weight on what are *typically* seen as basic needs within the society. For instance, a spoiled millionaire in modern America who has developed extraordinary needs for material goods, and who is miserable for lack of billions, does not count as poor. And a monk who happens to be contented with his standard of living is poor nonetheless. Since the millionaire has more than enough to meet what would typically be seen as basic needs in modern America, he is not poor, regardless of the fact that his own needs are unmet, and he is miserable. (Behind this semantic fact there may lie the moral judgment that such a person does not deserve the sympathy implied by the label "poor." For could he not have made himself less vulnerable to frustration by staying in the cultural mainstream and not letting himself develop these needs in the first place?) And conversely for the monk: he counts as poor because a typical person in his position would consider his needs unmet, whether the monk does or not.

In theory, then, it should be possible to draw a line below which people count as poor in a given society, even granting that the point at which individuals feel the pinch of material shortages will vary. The poverty line for a particular society will be that level of consumption below which needs that are typically considered basic in that society are unmet.

An Absolute Standard of Basic Need Across Eras and Nations?

But given that there is in each society a poverty line that transcends differences in individuals' conceptions of basic need, is there also a poverty line that transcends the differences between nations and eras? As Bradley Schiller points out, in the United States in 1936 the ordinary understanding of basic needs implied that about one-third of America was poor, as President Franklin Roosevelt declared at the time, but by the more generous understanding of basic needs that prevails in America today, more than half of that 1936 population was poor.[5] Analogously, just about no one in modern Chuuk has material goods sufficient to meet what are typically seen as basic needs in modern America, but the majority does not see itself as poor, because the Chuukese culture has a lower standard than ours for meeting basic needs. The question raised is, must we always understand "poverty" as an abbreviation for "poverty by the standards of time x in place y"? or is there a way to look beyond the variations and speak of "true poverty"?

It is tempting to absolutize our own intuitions about what constitutes a basic need and simply declare the standards of the past too low and the standards of the future too high. On this way of thinking, some supposedly nonpoor people in 1936 — having median incomes but lacking indoor plumbing and electricity — were actually poor, but they did not know it. An especially welcome corollary of this approach is that the just-below-the-future-poverty-line denizens of a future, super-prosperous America — with their reliable cars, their swimming pools, and their three-week vacations — turn out to be not really poor. This corollary is welcome because it is, in simple fact, hard to care about these future people's situation. (One person's frank comment was that the most he would be willing to do to help them would be to send them a message in a time capsule telling them that they are not so badly off.) We probably feel more comfortable rationalizing our indifference to them by saying that they will not really be poor than we do rational-izing our indifference by saying that they will poor, but we do not care. Yet tempting as it may be to absolutize our own intuitions about basic need, it is indefensible because what, after all, is special about our intuitions, as opposed to those of people in the past or the future? Certainly we cannot claim that our intuitions are more typical. In fact, it makes little sense to appeal to what the world's nations and eras have typically considered basic needs, for these conceptions are too diverse.

In the end, there seems to be no way to get around saying that "poverty" is always short for "poverty in place x and time y," and what it means is "having insufficient resources to meet what are typically seen as basic needs in that place and time." This is the best we can do in defining poverty, even if it leaves us in the uncomfortable position of having to say that we do not care much about some of the poverty that exists in richer times and places than our own. Note that to accept this definition is not to grant that "poverty" is ambiguous. Compare the word "edible." "Edible" is not ambiguous just because what horses can digest is different from what humans can digest.

What "edible" is is elliptical: the claim that something is edible is always short for "edible by such-and-such a species," but it means the same thing in each context. Likewise, poverty judgments are not ambiguous but elliptical, and once they are fleshed out the meaning is perfectly singular.

Given This Definition of Poverty, Where Is the Poverty Line in the United States Today?

What is the level of resources below which people are unable to meet what are typically seen as basic needs in modern America? and is there a practical earmark for identifying this level as it changes? Obviously no level of consumption can count as adequate if it fails to meet the physiological needs of the human animal for such things as food, clothing, and shelter, and what that level is has been carefully studied. The U.S. government's official answer is the federal poverty threshold. In 2005, that threshold was $10,160 for a single person under age sixty-five, $13,145 for a two-person household under age sixty-five — less than twice the amount for a single person owing to economies of scale — $19,971 for a family of four, and so forth.[6] The debatable aspects of this official poverty threshold have been exhaustively treated in several standard works on poverty and will not be pursued here.[7] They include the question whether it is still valid to assume, as the original drawers of the poverty threshold assumed, that overall physical needs can be met with an income of just three times what is needed for food, given that food accounts for a smaller fraction of the typical budget than it did when the official threshold was defined. A second issue is whether the use of the family as the unit of analysis is appropriate at a time when cohabiting couples and other nontraditional groupings are becoming more prevalent. For instance, it is arguably a weakness of the official poverty standard that it treats a cohabiting couple with $20,000 in total income as made up of poor individuals, while it treats a married couple with $12,600 as nonpoor. However, the technical problems of saying exactly what income suffices for meeting basic physiological needs will not concern us here. They are moot.

They are moot because, while the official poverty threshold is useful for research and policy development, it is not the real line between poverty and nonpoverty in modern America. Poverty is a matter of meeting or not basic needs for material goods, as ordinarily understood. Key, then, is discovering the ordinary understanding of basic needs in a given time and place. The best way to do this is surely to ask people. When this has been done, the poverty line that emerges for contemporary America is much higher than the official, physiological-needs-based poverty threshold. The likeliest explanation of this difference is not that the scientists and the general public disagree about what it takes to meet physiological needs. It is that the public recognizes the existence of nonphysiological basic needs as well, such as the needs for standing, respect, and social inclusion, which are hard for those at the official poverty threshold to fulfill, given the big (and growing) gap between the median income and the official poverty threshold. The official poverty threshold seems to be just too far from the income at the middle of the pack for people at that level to feel that they are full members of society.

In fact, the income required to meet what the public sees as basic needs in the United States is about half of the median income for the society, which is several thousand dollars more than the official poverty line today. Moreover, as John Iceland has shown, this holds not only for the present but also over time. That is, the perceived (and hence real) poverty line has roughly coincided with half the median income for at least the past fifty years.[8]

2

Behavioral Factors in Poverty

Evils can be combated by prevention or cure. Some evils, like AIDS, can be prevented but not cured, and some, like grief at the loss of loved ones, can be cured but not prevented. Poverty, like most evils, can be combated both ways. The focus of this book is curing poverty. It considers the situation of people who are already poor, such as children born into poor families. As I indicated in the preface, their poverty often persists. Why, and what can be done to help?

The project of relieving poverty has to start with an understanding of the factors that keep poor people poor or make them even poorer. The results arrived at in the first chapter may seem to imply that these factors cannot very well be common across eras and nations. After all, if "poverty" refers to very different material conditions in different times and places, how likely is it that the persistence and worsening of poverty will have a common set of causes? But surprisingly enough, a number of the factors that help explain the persistence of poverty transcend time and place. Specifically, certain ways of acting, certain things that poor people do more often than others, help to keep them poor or worsen their poverty.

To avert confusion, I hasten to stress that focusing on "behavioral" factors is not prejudging the issue of who or what is ultimately responsible for the persistence of poverty. In particular, to identify behavioral factors in poverty is not to lay the blame for poverty at the door of the poor themselves. The question of ultimate responsibility will be discussed in later chapters. My claim in this chapter is a relatively narrow one. I want to argue only that behaviors found disproportionately among the poor in many times and many places are important proximate causes of the continuation and worsening of their poverty—causes that come close to poverty itself in the chain of cause and effect, whatever factors may lie further back in the chain.

Five patterns that have been common among the poor in many times and places, then, and that have played a role in keeping them poor or making them poorer are

1. not working much for pay;
2. not getting much education;
3. not saving for a rainy day;
4. abusing alcohol; and
5. taking risks with the law.

Nineteenth-Century America

Among those who have been struck by the links between poverty and these patterns, or at least most of them, are nineteenth-century American social reformers. American reformers who attempted to "fight poverty with virtue" consistently associated poverty with "indolence, improvidence, and intemperance." These are obviously judgmental labels. But we do not have to go along with the reformers' assignment of blame in order to take seriously their perceptions. What they saw, minus the moralistic spin, was that poor people were likelier than nonpoor people not to work ("indolence"), likelier not to cushion themselves against the possibility of hard(er) times to come ("improvidence"), and likelier to get incapacitated by alcohol ("intemperance"); and moreover, that poor people would have been less poor or not poor at all if they had acted differently in these respects.[1]

As for not getting much education, the nineteenth-century reformers saw this as a species of indolence, which was one of their recognized causes of poverty. Not getting much education was for them laziness about the special work of learning that would increase the rewards of later work for pay. The historian Michael B. Katz says that nineteenth-century charity workers linked success with the sending of one's children to school and teaching them manners, and the reformer Robert Hartley is quoted as saying in 1855 that poverty is worst for those who have gotten little job training.[2]

Cultures of Poverty

Most of these behaviors were identified as factors in the persistence of poverty also in the poor urban areas of Mexico and Puerto Rico in the middle of the twentieth century. The field work of the famous anthropologist Oscar Lewis inclined him to the view that these urban communities were characterized by common acceptance of "chronic unemployment and underemployment," "low levels of literacy and education," "absence of savings" — perhaps related to the infrequent use of banks — and property crime; and that the dire condition of the inhabitants was partly traceable to these community values. For this reason, he called these communities "cultures of poverty."[3]

The United States Today

Another setting of significance is the contemporary United States. Evidence confirms two key points: all five behaviors are commoner among poor people in the United States than among nonpoor people, and the behaviors play a significant role in sustaining or worsening their poverty. The quality and quantity of this evidence are reasons to focus on it. But in paying special heed to the case of contemporary America, I do not mean to suggest that the United States is a special case. My larger point is just the reverse: that whether poverty means a few hundred dollars a year or twenty thousand in a given setting, the same behavioral factors crop up as important proximate causes.[4] The following are some key pieces of evidence regarding the United States.

Work

Of the five behaviors identified above, working for pay has gotten the most attention in recent poverty research. Let me start with whether poor people are likelier not to work than nonpoor people. U.S. Census data show just that: poor people are likelier not to work. In the year 2000, for instance, 51 percent of poor people between the ages of eighteen and sixty-four did not work at all, as compared with 14 percent of people who were not poor. In other words, complete nonwork was more than three times as common among the working-age poor as it was among the working-age nonpoor. A similar conclusion holds if one interprets "working" to mean "working full-time, year-round" rather than "working at all." Fully 85 percent of working-age poor people did not work full-time, year-round, as compared with just 38 percent of the people who were not poor. Putting it the other way around, working full-time, year-round was less than a quarter as common among the poor as among the nonpoor — 15 percent versus 62 percent. A similar conclusion obtains if one looks not at all people of working age but at subpopulations. Of fathers in two-parent families with children, for instance, nearly a quarter of those who were poor did not work for pay at all, while nonwork was practically unknown among fathers who were not poor, at 3 percent. Without prejudging the debate about the reasons for the difference in work behavior between the poor and the nonpoor, one can safely say that poor people work less, and the difference is big.[5]

That leaves the question whether the disparity makes a difference. Does not working or not working much help explain the poverty of the poor? Not surprisingly, the answer is yes. The surprise, if there is one, is just how big a difference working seems to make. Some indication can be gotten from correlational data. Of all persons sixteen and over who did not work at all in 2001, 21 percent were poor, whereas only 2.6 percent of this group who worked full-time, year-round were poor. In other words, working full-time, year-round, as opposed to not working at all, was associated with an *eightfold* difference in the probability of being poor — the difference between a one in five probability and a one in forty probability.[6] Granted, the question of causation is not definitively answered by such facts. For instance, it could be that full-time, year-round workers are rarely poor not because this amount of work is a reliable ticket out of poverty but because the people who could not escape poverty even by working full-time, year-round know this and do not bother to try.

But more sophisticated statistical studies make the stronger, causal claim — that whether and how much one works is a factor in whether one is poor. One 2003 simulation estimates that if all nonelderly and nondisabled heads of families with children worked full-time at their present wages, or at the wages they could earn based on their education and other factors, the fraction of the U.S. population living below the poverty line would fall from 13 percent to 7.5 percent. That would succeed in reducing the group of Americans who live in poverty by more than ten million.[7]

Not Getting Much Education

Social science supports the common observation that early exits from the educational process are more common among poor young people in the United States than among young people who are not poor. According to the National Center for Educational Statistics, in the year 2001, the high school dropout rate of people ages sixteen to twenty-four from families in the lowest income quartile was 21 percent; in the next quartile, it was 13 percent; in the third quartile, 8 percent; and the dropout rate of young people from families in the highest income quartile was just 4 percent. In short, young people from the poorest families are more than five times as likely to drop out of high school as young people from the richest families are.[8]

Moreover, with dropping out as with not working, the difference makes a difference. The early exits of young people from poor families make it more likely that they will be poor as adults. Census data from the year 2000 for persons twenty-five years and older provide some evidence. Adults who did not finish high school had a 22 percent probability of being poor, while even high school graduates with no college education at all had only a 9 percent chance of being poor.[9]

Here again, correlation does not prove causation. It could be that low educational attainment plays no role in limiting earnings, but rather stems from personal qualities such as lack of diligence that also serve to limit earnings. But granted that this is a theoretical possibility, most students of the issue believe that educational attainment differences play some causal role in earnings differences, even if other differences between people partially account for both. The consensus is that education is a process of acquiring tools that increase a student's productivity — and hence the wages that student can earn as an adult. From this perspective, studying is work that makes one's own later paid work pay better.

More disputed is the question, just what fraction of earnings differences can be explained by educational attainment differences? Controlling for other common differences between the more educated and the less educated — for instance, aptitude and motivation — one well-known study reported that differences in years of education accounted for about 15 percent of the earning differences between people, which puts education far, far ahead of years of work experience, test scores, motivation to achieve, and several other likely looking variables in explaining earnings differences.[10]

One word on a related subject may be in order. Having children early and out of wedlock is not among the poverty-causing behaviors I have chosen to focus on. That is because it is not as global or as perennial as the other factors on our list. But it is doubtless a big factor in poverty in the United States today. So its own roots are certainly an important area for investigation. Conjecture about the recent upsurge of early parenting has been wide-ranging. Observers have postulated shifts in morality, culture, and even biology. But there is another possibility. Could it be that the attractiveness of early parenthood has not changed in absolute terms, but that there is more of it because the attractiveness of staying in school to build intellectual capital, which is its main alternative, has in some quarters diminished? In other words, perhaps the brakes of morality and culture and the spur of biology have all maintained their relative importance, while the brake of intellectual capital accumulation has weakened. To the degree that early, out-of-wedlock parenting is itself a factor in poverty, this would make the issue of leaving school doubly urgent for antipoverty policy.

Not Saving for a Rainy Day

The common failure of poor people to save for a rainy day — or in their case, an even rainier day — appears to leave them unprotected from the vagaries of economic fate. Therefore it seems to be a factor in their suffering episodes of especially low consumption. Different saving behavior on their part during the usual drizzle of their economic lives would protect them from being drenched during the downpours. Curiously, thrift does not seem to figure much in the contemporary conversation about poverty, which focuses much more on willingness to work and on the importance of intact families, but evidence suggests it should.[11]

First, it is well documented that brief dips in income are a common feature of economic life in the United States. One study found that about one-fourth of Americans lived in families that were below the official poverty line for at least one year in the decade 1969–78, while only 2.6 percent lived in families that were poor in eight of those years. Ratcheting up the poverty line by 25 percent does not change this relationship much: it simply bumps up the number of people who were poor for one or more years to about one-third and bumps up the number of people who were poor in eight of those years to 5.1 percent.[12] It is a fair inference that these dips are not confined to the lives of the nonpoor. If sunny stretches are interrupted by rain, presumably drizzly stretches are interrupted by cloudbursts as well. Moreover, the dips experienced by the poor, when they come, seem no less deep than those experienced by the nonpoor. Thus a recent study showed that people who normally earn in the higher brackets and people who normally earn in the lower brackets lose similar proportions of their income from becoming unemployed.[13]

But second, poor people are less likely to save than nonpoor people. In 2004, for instance, saving was practiced by only 34 percent of families in the lowest income quintile, roughly coinciding with the poor part of the population. By comparison, 44 percent of the second quintile, 54 percent of the third quintile, 69 percent of the fourth quintile, and more than 78 percent of the highest quintile saved.[14] Obviously, the poorest people tend to have less protection from the rains, or in their case the inundations, when they come. This is reflected in the fact that people whose education leads us to expect them to be high earners, namely, college graduates, have assets equivalent to 1.2 times the income lost from unemployment and consequently spend not a penny less than usual on durable consumer goods while unemployed; by contrast, those whose education leads us to expect them to be low earners, namely, high school dropouts, have assets amounting to just 5 percent of lost income and consequently spend fifty-three cents less on consumer durables for every dollar of income lost on account of unemployment.[15]

It would seem, then, that in many cases modest saving by poor people in their less bad years could keep their consumption from plummeting deep into the poverty range in their lower-income years. For instance, someone whose annual income is usually twenty thousand dollars, but whose income falls to ten thousand dollars one year in each decade, could in principle level the sum available for consumption each year at nineteen thousand dollars by putting aside one thousand dollars in each of her higher earning years. To the extent that brief spells of extremely low income cause poor people to suffer exceptionally low consumption, it looks like a small change in saving behavior could make a big difference to the amount of felt poverty. Whether this would be prudent remains to be seen. But on the surface it seems possible.

Abusing Alcohol

The abuse of alcohol presents some unique complications. One cannot say flatly that poor people in the United States drink more than nonpoor people. Before beginning to compare drinking by poor people and nonpoor people, researchers have to draw some careful distinctions. Are we interested in the relation between poverty and someone's ever having had a drink, or between poverty and someone's having had a few drinks in the past year, or between poverty and the number of drinks someone has in a week, or between poverty and the number of drinks someone has on a day when he or she drinks? Given that what we care about ultimately is the relation between poverty and alcohol *abuse,* the last of these is probably the most important, and researchers have in fact asked how poverty is related to the number of drinks that people who drink at least monthly consume on a day when they drink. It turns out that poor people drink a great deal more than nonpoor people when they drink. For instance, on days when they drink, males who participate in the Food Stamp program, which is limited to low-income people, consume an average of 5.8 alcoholic drinks, and males who are eligible but do not participate consume an average of 5.1 drinks. By contrast, males whose income is high enough to make them ineligible for the program drink only 3.4 drinks. If we take the standard definition of binge drinking—five drinks at a sitting for a male — it is fair to infer that poor men typically binge when they drink, whereas nonpoor men do not. There are also large differences between the drinking behavior of poor and nonpoor females, poor women being much likelier to drink at a binge or abuse level. Poverty predicts abusive drinking among those who drink.[16]

But does the abusive drinking of poor people who drink help to account for their being poor? A 1996 study which took the number of drinks that someone drinks in a week as its independent variable concluded that heavy drinking raises the likelihood of two intermediate factors that in turn affect income: developing coronary artery disease, which is often disabling, and weekly hours worked. Common observation suggests yet a third income-lowering consequence of heavy drinking: a drop in productivity while actually on the job. Hangovers, not to mention being drunk on the job, are like schooling in reverse, subtracting from the sufferer's human capital, if only temporarily. As to the magnitude of these effects, the study concludes that "the effect of alcohol consumption on earnings is statistically significant, but not as significant as traditional human capital variables such as education or age."[17]

Is this consistent with the opinions of poor people themselves? I have not found evidence on whether poor people themselves consider alcohol abuse specifically to be a significant factor in poverty, but a 2001 survey did find that poor people consider "drug abuse" — not further defined but presumably including alcohol abuse for some respondents — to be a significant factor. In fact, the survey asked respondents to identify the most important cause of poverty, listing ten options: drug abuse; medical bills; too many jobs being part-time or low wage; too many single-parent families; a shortage of jobs; the welfare system; too many immigrants; poor people lacking motivation; decline in moral values; and poor quality of public schools. Among respondents who were *themselves* poor (by the official standard), drug abuse was far and away the winner, 22 percent identifying it as the most important cause. (Too many jobs being part-time or low wage was next, at 17 percent.) It may well be, then, that many poor people not only agree with the research that alcohol is a significant cause of poverty but actually rate it a more serious cause than the empirical research does—ahead of the quality of public education, for instance.[18]

Just as poor people disproportionately put their health and therefore their income at risk by abusive drinking, so do they take and accept other health risks with negative consequences for their income. For instance, W. Kip Viscusi states that poor people are more likely to smoke and to become obese than nonpoor people. As for acceptance of health risks, whether traceable either to one's own behavior or to fate, there is a well-known correlation between low income and not insuring, which is to say, not paying a relatively small sum to be protected from owing a much larger sum in the eventuality one needs expensive medical care. The U.S. Census Bureau reports that in recent years poor people in the United States have been about twice as likely to be totally uncovered by insurance, despite the existence of Medicaid and Medicare, as people who are not poor. Judging by the fact that in the 2001 survey, 74 percent of people who were themselves poor identified medical bills as a major cause of poverty, it seems fair to infer that accepting this risk has made the poverty of some poor people significantly worse.[19]

Taking Risks with the Law

Committing property crime is, from the criminal's standpoint, the taking of a risk with the potential upside of monetary gain and the potential downside of incarceration, with accompanying loss of income. Recent empirical studies confirm that property crime is "significantly aggravated by poverty."[20] Less often investigated is the reverse causality—whether property crime tends to impoverish those who commit it. One careful study of criminals in California, Michigan, and Texas in 1988 found that for most criminal specialties a busy schedule of crime paid less per year than the work the criminals could have expected to do, given their poor educations and other qualities, after subtracting from the criminals' work year the period of involuntary unemployment that is incarceration. For instance, a busy "generalist" criminal was found to make about fifty-seven hundred dollars a year during the time he was not in jail, whereas a legitimate minimum-wage job would have paid about seventy-nine hundred dollars after taxes. Note that even netting seventy-nine hundred dollars would have meant being in or near poverty at the time—the line in 1988 was about fifty-five hundred dollars for an individual and twelve thousand dollars for a family of four. Hence the study supports the generalization that criminal careers make those who engage in them even poorer in the long run than they would have been with available regular employment, while introducing a considerable variation in income over shorter periods.[21]

As bad as this makes career crime look, however, there is worse to come. After all, the study does not even try to come to terms with the question of how much someone is impoverished by incarceration in itself, which is an outcome that repeat offenders should and do expect to suffer. To what level of "regular poverty" should a year spent partly behind bars be compared? To some observers, the material deprivations of time behind bars seem almost incalculably severe, especially considering their impact on nonphysical basic needs for respect, social inclusion, and so forth. From this standpoint too it seems that career crime causes poverty, assuming, of course, that there is a significant risk of being incarcerated. Which there is: on the low end, an averagely active swindler can expect to spend 45 days per year in prison, while a busy car thief can expect to spend no fewer than 274 days per year in prison.[22] For those concerned about poverty, then, the deep roots of the risks taken by criminals are a proper topic of study.

Can These Behaviors Provide a Lever for Relieving Poverty?

Aligning the behavior of the poor more closely with societal norms by causing them to work more, stay in school longer, save more, drink less, and commit fewer property crimes would have a positive impact on their economic condition. It is tempting to conclude, then, that opponents of poverty should use their time and energy to try to make this alignment happen. What is more, it is tempting to conclude that reformers should devote the biggest share of their time and energy to changing those behaviors with the biggest impact on poverty, such as nonwork. This is exactly the logic of a recent policy proposal that begins by showing that increasing full-time work and marriage would have a big impact on the poverty rate in the United States and concludes by recommending "strategies that encourage work and marriage" as particularly "effective."[23]

But this reasoning leaves out a key step. Some of the problematic behaviors may not be changeable, at least not by reformers. And even if they can all be affected by public policies to some degree, those with the most potential impact on poverty may be less tractable than other behaviors having a smaller potential impact. For instance, it may turn out to be easier to affect poor people's persistence in school than to affect their work behavior, even granting that work behavior is a more significant behavioral factor in poverty than school persistence. In that case, would the greater potential impact be worth the extra difficulty of affecting work behavior?

Essential for answering such questions is identifying the causes of the poverty-causing behaviors themselves. What makes poor people less likely to work, finish school, save, drink moderately, and obey the law than nonpoor people? and how hard are these root causes to alter through the use of the instruments of public policy? The hope is, of course, that some of these root causes will turn out to be promising targets for intervention, when the likely impact of the intervention on the behavior is factored in with the likely impact of changing the behavior itself.

3

Some Theories

Poor people are likelier than nonpoor people to do certain things that tend, in fact, to keep them poor or make them poorer. They are likelier than nonpoor people to spend their time in unpaid activities, drop out of school, fail to save, drink too much when they drink, and break the law. But why? It's an important question. Any effort to relieve poverty by changing these behaviors has to start by understanding them.

There are a number of familiar theories.[1] One way to classify these theories is by whether they treat the behaviors in question as stemming from psychological dysfunctions. Note that being dysfunctional in this sense is not the same thing as having preferences that happen to be socially disapproved of, such as a strong preference for leisure over income. Preferring leisure is often disparaged as a kind of flaw, but it is not a flaw in the sense that a dysfunction is. Dysfunctions are not preferences, even socially disapproved ones, but conditions that get in the way of realizing preferences.

The dysfunction approach blames nonwork and the other poverty-prolonging/poverty-worsening behaviors on several problems in particular. One is apathy. Others are fragmentation of the self, which leads to short time horizons, and weakness of the will.[2] Alternatives to dysfunctionalism naturally deny that psychological dysfunctions are key factors in causing these behaviors. Instead, they trace the behaviors to external circumstances, such as restricted opportunity and bad public policy. Or they trace them to inner qualities that are not dysfunctions (in the above sense), such as the preference for leisure or a taste for the suspense and excitement of risk taking.

Dysfunction Theories

The premise of the dysfunction theories is that the nonwork, school quitting, nonsaving, excessive drinking, and criminal acts of poor people are satisfaction-inefficient. They fail to wring the greatest possible long-run satisfaction for the agent from the time, energy, money, and other resources available. It is this alleged inefficiency that short time horizons, lack of willpower, and the other dysfunctions are brought in to explain. A word is in order here about terminology. Social scientists sometimes use the term "irrationality" for what I am calling satisfaction-inefficiency. Thus they sometimes call wasteful or self-defeating conduct irrational. By the same token, the project of showing that certain apparently inefficient behavior is really efficient after all is sometimes called rationalizing the behavior. There is little harm in following this usage, as I sometimes will, as long as it is kept in mind that, strictly speaking, inefficiency is a quality of acts, whereas irrationality is a quality of agents — and indeed one that often explains inefficiency.

But what is the argument that these patterns are inefficient? The reasoning cannot very well be that the behaviors waste satisfaction simply insofar as they sustain or worsen poverty. After all, for all I have said so far, poverty could be a small price to pay for plentiful leisure, freedom from the rigors of school, and uninhibited drinking. And for all I have said so far, intervals of deep poverty, caused by nonsaving and crime, could be a small price to pay for intervals of not-so-deep poverty. That would make the five behaviors satisfaction-efficient on balance rather than wasteful.

The Missing Piece of the Inefficiency Argument

Something like the following has to be assumed to reach the conclusion that the conduct in question is inefficient:

> Poor people consume little in the way of goods and services. But it is an old and true observation that the less of a good one consumes, the greater the satisfaction one gets from a little bit of it, and conversely that the more of a good one consumes, the less the satisfaction one gets from a little bit of it. Who would deny that a single dollar means more to someone who is struggling to put food on the table than it would mean to her if she had a million other dollars besides? Surely, then, the dollars that a poor person can earn by working will be sweet dollars indeed, when compared to the dollars of the rich. So poor people should regard working for pay as very worthwhile. When poor people do not work, they pass up the chance to increase satisfaction on balance. As Lawrence Mead says of nonwork, "The puzzle is that poor adults seem less responsive to economic incentives than the better off, even though they need money more."[3]

By the same token [continues the inefficiency argument] *schoolwork,* which enhances earning power, is especially valuable to poor people, seeing that they have so much satisfaction to gain by an increase in income. So it is counterproductive for them to drop out of school early, as a disproportionate number do. And heavy drinking by poor people is yet another waste of potential satisfaction, given the extra income that those whose drinking is moderate can expect to earn, and the great satisfaction that is derived from extra income by those whose incomes are small. In a nutshell, the lost income from not working, not building one's earning capacity through education, and heavy drinking is bound to cost the poor an inordinate amount of satisfaction, and the fact that poor people so often do these things represents a departure from the usual human pursuit of self-interest.

The apparent wastefulness of nonsaving and crime rests on much the same logic:

We know that a dollar means more to someone when it is one of few than it would if it were one of many. Presumably, then, a dollar will mean more to someone on his poorer days than on his richer ones. This fact should motivate a self-interested person to level his spending of any given amount of money across time. After all, the extra dollar that is enjoyed on a boom day will yield less satisfaction than it would have yielded on a bust day, when it would have been one of a smaller number of dollars. To take an analogy, if you have two ice cream sandwiches and two successive dinners for which you need dessert, it would make more sense to eat one at each meal than to eat them both at one meal, because the second ice cream sandwich at a sitting is usually not as satisfying as the first. To avoid wasting satisfaction, then, people should smooth out the economic peaks and valleys of life by saving, and they should keep from introducing peaks and valleys needlessly by committing crimes. Poor people disproportionately waste satisfaction both ways.

In fact [concludes the inefficiency argument], the wastefulness of nonsaving and crime is even greater than this. Failure to save causes not only uneven consumption but also reduced total consumption, owing to the loss of the investment returns that are normally available from savings. And the cash flow of a career criminal is not only variable but smaller in total than that of a comparable legitimate worker, as we saw in chapter 2. But from what we have already seen, these sacrifices in total income will burden the poor even more heavily than the nonpoor. So there are really two reasons for poor people to save and obey the law. This makes it doubly counterproductive not to.

Here, then, is the puzzle of poverty. And the response of dysfunctionalism, again, is not to dispute that poor people depart more often than nonpoor people from the usual human pattern by behaving inefficiently. The response is to acknowledge this as a fact and attribute it to psychological dysfunction. The main versions of this general hypothesis are as follows.

Apathy

One version says that poor people disproportionately adopt satisfaction-sacrificing patterns because poor people are more often apathetic. It is not that their preferences are unusual, but that the preferences they would otherwise have are suppressed by a patholog-ical condition. So in effect they are indifferent. They are not moti-vated to throw themselves into work or school. They do little to mitigate the economic ups and downs of fate. And so on. And the reason they are indifferent is that they are despairing or depressed. Beneath the poverty problem there lies, in effect, a public mental health problem.[4]

The dysfunctional apathy theory is not to be confused with the idea that many poor people prefer to take life as it comes. Apathy is not a sort of mellowness but a pitiable condition closely tied to the inability to enjoy life—even by taking it as it comes. Unlike being mellow, being apathetic is something no one could want, which is reflected in the fact that people pay Buddhist teachers to help them go with the flow and psychiatrists to help them overcome apathy. Nor is dysfunctional apathy the same thing as asking very little from life to avoid being disappointed. To prefer not to be disappointed is, after all, to prefer.

Supporters of the apathy theory account for the alleged apathy in various ways. Decades ago Michael Harrington argued that "there is, in a sense, a personality of poverty, a type of human being produced by the grinding, wearing life of the slums . . . hopeless and passive, yet prone to bursts of violence."[5] A more recent explanation says that poor people "give up" because of frustration at the failure of their early efforts to help themselves. They suffer from what is sometimes called learned helplessness. Another version ties self-indifference to low self-respect—"I am so worthless that I am not entitled to have preferences"—brought on by early mistreatment at the hands of au-thority figures such as parents and teachers, who have been credited with having wisdom on account of their power. Other proponents cite existential or religious despair, or depression based in neurochemistry. Naturally each explanation implies its own countermeasures. Suggested fixes range from antidepression medication to psychotherapy to religious revival.

Interpreted as a complete account of the motivations or nonmotivations behind the poverty-linked conduct, the apathy theory is open to serious objections. Even the figures quoted by Harrington do not invite the wide generalization of his theory: 1,659 cases of treated psychiatric illness per 100,000 in the lowest socioeconomic class.[6] For another thing, the apathy theory leads us to expect an affectless style of behavior among those poor people who engage in the poverty-linked conduct, which is by no means universally observed. No doubt some poor people who do not work are victims of serious depression, and some alcohol abuse seems to be self-medication for depression. But having a baby during one's teens is not necessarily a gloomy affair. Likewise, spending like there is no tomorrow is often pretty lively while it lasts. Recall Aesop's fable about imprudence, in which one creature saves corn for the winter while another does not and goes hungry. It seems significant that while Aesop's symbol of prudence is the ant, his symbol of improvidence is the grasshopper, a creature that cavorts around and chirps. Surely apathy cannot be the whole answer.

The Fragmented Self

This view explains the supposed wastefulness of the behaviors differently. Rather than seeing poor people as apathetic, it claims that poor people are, more often than nonpoor people, disintegrated. In the terminology of nineteenth-century German philosophy, they are alienated from themselves. For instance, the poor person who consumes unevenly by failing to save underserves his future self, at some cost to his long-run satisfaction, because he sees his future self almost as a distinct person, one with whom he does not fully identify. Likewise the poor person who does not work underweights his appetite for earnings, sacrificing overall satisfaction, because he experiences his desire for income weakly, as if it belonged to someone else.

How do proponents of the fragmented-self theory explain the supposed fact that self-alienation afflicts the poor more than the non-poor? One view is that poor people are less likely to see themselves holistically because they are more dominated by forces that fragment the self into facets and phases. In particular, social theorists in the tradition running from Friedrich Schiller through Karl Marx to Norman O. Brown and Herbert Marcuse have blamed the fragmented self on modern social and economic structures, especially the capitalist workplace, that naturally distort the psyches of the weak more than the psyches of the strong. Because capitalism forces the poor to subordinate so much of themselves in each context, and because they are valued only temporarily, as long as they are productive, poorer individuals lose the sense of themselves as integrated and persisting selves. No wonder, then, that when they allocate their energies between work and play, they so often treat their own needs for earnings almost as if they were the needs of another person, or that when they budget, they so often treat their own future interests almost as if they were the interests of another person.

The diagnosis implies the therapy. In order to overcome the over- and underweighting of parts and phases of the self that supposedly lead to the behaviors in question, society must promote the sense of the self as an integrated whole. Note that pursuing this goal is consistent with thinking that self-identification and self-alienation are innate. Aesop's own case shows this. For presumably his point in allegorizing prudence and imprudence as instinct-driven natural creatures like the ant and the grasshopper was that these qualities are innate. But if he did not think imprudence could be overcome, why would he have bothered telling his fable?

From the standpoint of the tradition of Schiller and Marx, promoting self-integration means nothing less than reforming of the problematic social and economic structures that fragmented the self in the first place. A more conventional cure focuses on methods like those used to promote a sense of connection with others. For instance, where the unsympathetic may be prodded to imagine themselves in the shoes of others by descriptions of the others' inner lives, the imprudent may be prodded to imagine themselves in their own future shoes, as it were, by vivid descriptions of how things will seem to them in the future.

Interpreted as a general account of the poverty-linked conduct, the fragmented-self view, like the apathy theory, is open to serious objections. For one thing, it leads us to expect that poor people who vary consumption regard their future interests casually, like Aesop's grasshopper. For supposedly these interests are being viewed as the interests of a quasi-other. But on the contrary, uneven consumption on the part of the poor is often serious and deliberate. In chapter 5, I will discuss a particularly interesting ancient example of this from Herodotus. A contemporary example from the developing world, noted by Tibor Scitovsky in *The Joyless Economy,* is poor families' common practice of deliberately depriving themselves over long periods for the sake of a feast at the end, for instance, a wedding feast.[7]

Another problem with the fragmented-self theory is that from a positivist standpoint, at least, the very notion of a "normal preference for income, weakly felt" makes little sense. For what scientifically measurable behavior can possibly differentiate a normally strong preference for income, weakly felt, from a preference for income that is simply weak? But if the poor person's normal but weakly felt desire for income boils down to nothing more than a weak desire for income, then his so-called indulgence in leisure does not necessarily represent a sacrifice of overall satisfaction in the first place. This line of thinking pushes the self-alienation theory very close to the solution of the puzzle that sees nonwork and the other questionable behaviors as perfectly rational strategies for satisfying preferences that happen to be atypical. (I will come back to the atypical preferences theory in a moment.)

Weakness of the Will

The last psychological dysfunction cited by those who regard the poverty-prolonging/worsening conduct as inefficient is weakness of the will. This is sometimes known by its Greek name, *akrasia*. As contrasted with the earlier theories, this one locates the problem further down the causal chain leading to action: not in the absence of preferences and not in the distancing of one's preferences, but in the failure to enact one's preferences. For instance, poor people who consume "like there is no tomorrow" are seen as wanting to avoid the sacrifice of their long-term interests that comes from neglecting tomorrow, but as being unable to act on their preferences in the face of temptation. One proponent puts it as follows: "Ethnographers generally find that the poor endorse the same values as the better-off. They also want to work for a living, get through school, support their families, avoid trouble with the law, and so on. These professions appear sincere. But for obscure reasons, the poor often fail to do these things. Of course, most people fail to fulfill all their intentions in life, but for the poor that gap is unusually wide."[8]

On this version, reformers of the problematic behavior should be focusing not on relieving depression or reintegrating the self but on strengthening willpower. Suggested strategies have included tough-love public policies, exhortations, therapies, and medication.

The *akrasia* theory seems more robust as a general account of the behavior in question than the apathy theory and the fragmented-self theory. At least it is not defeated by the most famous objection against it. This is the claim, associated with Socrates, that weakness of the will is simply nonexistent. Socrates said that to know what is good for oneself is to do it. If someone does not do what is good for him, it must be because he does not know it is good for him. Seeming lapses of willpower are nothing but failures of belief and knowledge. For instance, someone who smokes while claiming to recognize and care about the dangers must in fact doubt either the risks to or the importance of health, regardless of what he says. But this is silly. Therapists sometimes get people to stop smoking without so much as mentioning the risks to health or the value of health, just by focusing on patients' lack of willpower and perhaps its roots in childhood.[9] Given that neither health risks nor the value of health are mentioned, it makes little sense to suppose that the therapies work by changing beliefs about smoking or the relative satisfactions drawn from smoking and health. It is more plausible to say that the therapies help people act in accordance with their preferences. But this is just to say that the patients were not doing that at the start. Weakness of the will must have been a factor. So weakness of the will is not a complete mirage after all.

A more obvious objection to the *akrasia* theory likewise fails to defeat it. We tend to think that the victory of impulse over willpower has to be dramatic and even explosive, like a straitlaced pair finally falling into each other's arms in a romantic movie. But don't poor people often engage in unpaid pursuits, drop out of school, spend all their income, and so forth in a steady and deliberate manner? So, runs the objection, *akrasia* cannot very well be the whole story. But this rebuttal depends on a mistaken impression about the process of succumbing to temptation, beautifully lampooned by J. L. Austin in his classic essay "A Plea for Excuses": "I am very partial to ice cream, and a bombe is served divided into segments corresponding one to one with the persons at High Table; I am tempted to help myself to two segments and do so, thus succumbing to temptation . . . But do I lose control of myself? Do I raven, do I snatch the morsels from the dish and wolf them down, impervious to the consternation of my colleagues? Not a bit of it. We often succumb to temptation with calm and even with finesse."[10] Perhaps the questionable conduct is simply the kind of victory of impulse over discipline described by Austin.

Other Doubts About Tracing the Poverty-Prolonging Behaviors to Dysfunction

Few will deny that poor people are sometimes apathetic, unconcerned about their future selves, impulsive, etc. But that is not the contested point. The psychological dysfunction approach claims that such weaknesses are widespread among the poor, explaining much or all of the behavior in question, while doubters concede only a limited number of cases. To the apathy version, for instance, the critic will say, "I will grant that poor people are sometimes apathetic, and this may account for some proportion of nonwork and of the other poverty-prolonging behaviors. But it is incorrect to generalize from these few bona fide cases."

Opponents of the dysfunction approach often suspect that supporters overgeneralize from a few clear cases of dysfunctional nonwork, nonsaving, and so on because they like the political corollary — paternalism. For the notion that poor people often act against their own interests on account of dysfunction seems to mean that the non-poor have a right, if not a duty, to regulate, treat, counsel, and otherwise guide poor people who do not work, finish school, save, etc. into different paths than they would otherwise choose, *for their own good*. And as for why supporters like paternalism in the first place, they like it, their critics suspect, because it rationalizes the primitive desire to control or shape the behavior of others: "We are justified in controlling the poor not just because we are in a position to do so, and we want to, but because it benefits *them*." In response, defenders of the dysfunction theory can say that critics refuse to acknowledge any but the most undeniable cases of dysfunction — refuse in fact to generalize legitimately — because they are biased in the opposite direction, in favor of a politically correct populism. Supposedly the critics are so eager to hold the poor blameless for their condition that they ratchet the hurdle for an acceptable inference too high. As with many ad hominem arguments that someone thinks something only because he likes its political implications, two can play at this game, and the dispute is inconclusive.

But a second doubt is not so easy to rebut. It says that dysfunction theories paint too complicated a picture of human behavior. For nature itself is simple and uniform. But this means that the parsimony of a theory about the natural world counts in favor of that theory. Less complicated accounts of phenomena should generally be preferred to more complicated ones. And there are in fact simpler accounts of the poverty-linked behaviors to be had than the dysfunction theories. Or so say opponents.

What is supposed to be complicated about the dysfunction theories? Not the hypothesis that some instances of not working, school quitting, not saving, and so on depart from the norms of human behavior by wasting possible satisfaction. The existence of a few anomalies in a class of phenomena is not itself an anomaly. What critics find too complicated is that dysfunctionalism draws an implausibly deep distinction right down the middle of the class of human behaviors. It makes a big portion goal-directed and a big portion not goal-directed. The supposed distinction can be described more exactly in the language of philosophy. On the one side are actions whose causes include someone's reasons for doing them. Such actions can be made sense of in terms of the agent's perceived interests, as when we say, "His reason for quitting was that he didn't get a raise, and the work was getting harder." On the other side of the line (one might almost say "tracks") lies a vast class of behaviors, linked to poverty, whose causes — depression, psychological dissociation, impulse — do not include someone's reasons for doing them. They cannot be understood as a means to the end of preference fulfillment. At least their causes do not include the reasons of an integral self. They happen for a reason, in other words, but no unitary agent has done them for a reason. They can be explained but not made sense of. This is reflected in the fact that when someone has quit on impulse, we can say, "He quit because of an impulse to do so," but not (usually), "His reason for quitting was that he had an impulse to do so." In the jargon of philosophy, these poverty-linked behaviors are held by dysfunctionalism to be nonteleological, like the motions of billiard balls, the breath-drawings and eye-blinkings of our bodies, and the erratic performances of those suffering from schizophrenia or multiple personality disorder. As such, they require a different kind of explanation than usual human behavior.

Critics of the dysfunction theories contend that the postulate of such a deep division right down the middle of the class of human behaviors fails the test of parsimony. A simpler and therefore better theory would find teleological rationality — a striving to maximize one's overall satisfaction — in almost all human behavior or in almost none. On the other hand, defenders of dysfunctionalism can reply with some justice that the parsimony objection does not hit all three forms of dysfunctionalism equally hard.[11] For the apathy version and the fragmented-self version, at least, trace the distinctive behavior of the poor back to distinctive circumstances, operating on a uniform human nature. The conditions faced by poor people would make apathetic or fragmented souls of us all. By contrast, the *akrasia* version of dysfunctionalism is more vulnerable to the parsimony objection because it usually traces the behavioral difference to a basic difference among agents. This is exemplified by Aesop, who represents weak-willed and self-disciplined behavior as manifesting the different natures of the grasshopper and the ant.

Alternatives to the Dysfunction Approach

Having raised such doubts, critics have put forward one of three alternatives. One theory says that most poor people who do not work, finish school, etc. fail to do these things because their opportunities are unduly limited. A second traces these behaviors to atypical preferences of the agents. Yet a third theory blames perverse incentives created by public policy. Significantly, these alternatives do not challenge every premise of the dysfunction approach. Opponents of dysfunctionalism agree with supporters of dysfunctionalism that *if* the poor people who behave in these ways had unrestricted opportunities; and *if* they had typical preferences; and *if* they faced neutral policy incentives, then their failures to work, save, etc. would be wasteful. Such failures would indeed be departures from the human norm of efficiency, calling for the postulate of dysfunctionality. But each of the three alternatives challenges one of the "ifs."

Restricted Opportunity[12]

The first of the alternatives says that poor people often engage in the poverty-prolonging and poverty-worsening behaviors not because they lack the will to do otherwise but because they lack the opportunity to do otherwise. The cause of nonwork, for instance, is not that poor nonworkers lack the desire to work but that there are not enough jobs for all the people who want them. An important variant says that even if there are enough jobs to go around overall, discrimination against such subpopulations as African Americans creates conditions in which there are not enough jobs for all the people in those discriminated-against groups who want them. This is held to explain the relatively high proportion of nonworking people in those discriminated-against groups. In short, the problematic behaviors are inevitable for some fraction of the population or the mistreated subpopulations, even if luck or other factors determine which particular individuals lose out. And just as nonworkers are those who lose out in the struggle for an insufficient number of jobs, dropouts are those who lose out in the competition for too few adequate educational opportunities; and poor nonsavers lack reliable ways to save; and poor criminals have no honest way to survive. (Alcohol abuse is not unavoidable, obviously. Rather it is usually seen as an indirect consequence of joblessness and low income.) So according to this theory the poor people in question make no decision that can be blamed on dysfunction.

But this view does not seem to be generally correct for the United States today, however applicable it may be elsewhere. The cause of the problematic conduct may not be dysfunction, but it does not appear to be absolute lack of opportunity either. For instance, sheer inability to find work does not seem to be pervasive or even common. To take just one indication, according to 1996 U.S. Census data covering nonworkers between ages twenty and sixty-four, only 8.2 percent of those lacking even a high school diploma cited inability to find work as their main reason for not working; and in the group with the hardest time finding work, African American nonworkers, less than one in seven gave inability to find work as their main reason for not working.[13]

Another point against the restricted opportunity theory also rests on survey data. If the restricted opportunity theory correctly explained most of the behavior in question, then restricted opportunity would be a major factor in poverty itself. But consider the opinions of poor people themselves about the causes of poverty. They are in a good position to know the causes, and they would, if anything, be expected to overblame opportunity restrictions for their poverty. But there is no consensus among poor people that restricted opportunity is the main cause of their poverty. In fact, according to the NPR/Kaiser/Kennedy School survey cited earlier, only 57 percent of poor people think the main cause of poverty is *any* factor lying beyond the control of poor people, whether opportunity restrictions or bad public policies or other. Parenthetically, in the specific case of saving, 89 percent of poor people in the same survey said that there was a bank convenient to them, hardly less than the 93 percent of respondents with incomes above the poverty line.[14]

Atypical Preferences

This view traces the problematic behaviors not to an internal dysfunction and not to an external condition of restricted opportunity, but to an internal condition that is not a dysfunction: poor people's allegedly unusual preferences. This theory grants that the poverty-prolonging/

worsening behaviors often seem to depart from ordinary human behavior by wasting a lot of possible satisfaction. But, says the theory, this is an illusion that arises because we overlook the difference between typical preferences and the preferences of poor people who engage in these behaviors. For instance, poor people who devote most of their time to unpaid pursuits generally do so because they get exceptional satisfaction from some alternative to work, such as staying home and raising their children, or because they suffer exceptional misery from working. This makes poverty the best available option for them. Thus even a seventh day in a row with the children, while it may be less satisfying than its six predecessors, will yield more net satisfaction than a first day spent working and earning. What would be irrational and wasteful under the circumstances would be to devote any days at all to paid work.[15]

A similar claim is made about seeming underallocations of time to education and the work of learning, which are notoriously distasteful to some people. As for seeming overallocations of money to certain time-slices of the self, that is, not saving, this might reflect a strong dislike for planning and a preference for living in the present. The life of habitual criminals has often been said to reflect a positive appetite for the forbidden and for the uncertainty of the outcomes. In short, all of the questionable, poverty-prolonging behaviors can be reseen as benefit-proportional and hence rational allocations if one takes into account the atypical preferences of the poor people who act in these ways. Or so this theory holds.

Atypical preference theorists who want to change the poverty-prolonging behaviors are obliged to defend their goal. For by hypothesis, working, finishing school, saving, and so on would cost the poor people whose behavior is to be changed some of the meager satisfaction they get from behaving as they do, as long as their preferences are what they are. One approach to justifying such interventions is to assert that these poor people literally do not know what is good for them, while the interveners do; but given the philosophical temper of our day, this position is rarely maintained, at least not in so many words. A commoner response is that the alternatives harm others. In cases like crime and quitting school, this is obvious enough, but there are gray areas. For instance, suppose that nonworking poor people prefer not to save, even though this means income variations, and suppose too that the middle class feels obliged to bail them out when they get into trouble. Is the financial burden of the bailouts that the middle class has, after all, *chosen* to bear the kind of "harm to society" that justifies their intervening in the behavior of the poor? Is "We will feel obliged to help them if they get in trouble" a legitimate justification for making poor people set aside part of their income for a rainy day or for doling out public assistance to them in equal portions each month, so that they cannot spend the money at the rate they choose?

The burden of justifying interventions to relieve poverty may be lighter on atypical preference theorists who want to change the behavior of the poor indirectly, by changing the atypical preferences. For once the poor people have the new preferences, the poverty-relieving behavior will actually increase their satisfaction on balance. This is the strategy of reformers who talk about the importance of "acculturating" poor people and helping them "assimilate" into the mainstream, and who decry "cultures of poverty" that spurn the work ethic. And as for justification, almost any burden placed on the wider society by the conduct of the poor, however small, may seem enough because once the preferences of the poor are changed everyone feels better off. Even a normative axiom like the axiom that a preference for hard work is just plain superior to — or better aligned with American traditions and values than — a strong preference for "leisure" may seem justification enough, since, again, once the preferences are changed, who is the loser?

Yet there are complications even here. Is preference reform so harmless if it divides generations, as children are taught to reject their parents' values? What if preference reform means that a way of life that contributes in other, noneconomic ways to the wider culture gets thrown into the famous American melting pot and vanishes? What if the new preferences are crude and materialistic? And is there not a point where reforming people's preferences starts to interfere with their very integrity as autonomous human beings?

These questions are doubtless deep. But whether they are also important depends on whether the atypical preferences theory that puts them on the table is a strong theory. One objection to the atypical preferences view is implicit in survey evidence. This evidence shows that large majorities of poor people and nonpoor people alike think poor people have the same "moral values" as other Americans, presumably including the work ethic. Moreover, as already reported, "ethnographers generally find that the poor endorse the same values as the better-off."[16] What is more, the metaprinciple of parsimony should incline us to seek explanations for the behavior that minimize the variables that have to be postulated. Unusual tastes and preferences, whether located in the individual or in the culture to which the individual conforms, are precisely the sort of variable we should try to omit from our explanation of poverty, absent overwhelming evidence for them.

Perverse Incentives Created by Public Policy

The third alternative to the dysfunction theory takes us back to the idea that external conditions make poverty-prolonging behavior rational. In this respect the third theory is like the restricted opportunity theory. But the external conditions being blamed in this case are not restricted opportunities but public policies that have been deliberately created to relieve poverty.

For instance, Charles Murray's *Losing Ground* popularized the view that the pre-1996, no-strings (or few strings) welfare system in the United States had actually prolonged the problem that policymakers were trying to relieve.[17] The idea was that giving things to poor people made it less necessary for them to work. This meant that, being rational, they worked less, and this in turn meant continued, indeed perpetual poverty and dependency. While some people contended that the harm that came from helping poor people in this way was less than the benefit—after all, no one was left completely unaided under this approach—there was wide acceptance of the basic notion that our national policy had made it reasonable for poor people to work a lot less. By the same token, public policy was said to have put downward pressure on people's efforts to raise future income by completing school, and on their motivation to save for a rainy day, and so on. In sum, public policy was supposed to have undermined the motivation of poor people to help themselves by behaving differently.

Once again, the survey data do not support this theory. For example, in the survey already cited, the welfare system was identified as the main cause of poverty by fewer poor people than any other of ten possible factors.[18] Perhaps this is to be expected, given their interests, but there is another problem too. Nonwork, school quitting, and other poverty-linked conduct are both perennial and common today in societies that lack robust systems of public assistance, such as those studied by Oscar Lewis. Must supporters of the perverse incentives theory say that the problematic behavior has different causes in different times and places? It is possible, but the principle of parsimony creates a presumption in favor of global and perennial explanations for global and perennial phenomena.

I have now considered six conventional explanations of the poverty-prolonging and poverty-worsening behaviors that are disproportionately engaged in by poor people. The first three purport to explain why poor people so often waste satisfaction, citing apathy, self-alienation, and lack of willpower. The second three contend that the conduct of the poor, no less than the conduct of the nonpoor, is generally satisfaction-efficient despite appearances to the contrary. To make sense of the conduct, this second trio of theories introduces collateral considerations — that poor people often face restricted opportunities, that they often have atypical preferences, that public policies confront them with perverse incentives. I have mentioned some objections to each of the six theories. These are not for the most part new objections. Generally they are points that the partisans of each make against rival theories. But in fact I think each of the six is open to a more radical objection as well. I will make this clear in chapter 5.

But first I am going to trace the historical development of the conventional argument that the conduct in question wastes satisfaction — what I called "the missing piece of the inefficiency argument" earlier in the present chapter. In tracing this history, I will highlight the key premises of the inefficiency argument and explain its logic more rigorously. This will lay the groundwork for a new refutation of the argument and a new case that the poverty-linked conduct is efficient after all.

4

A Closer Look at the
Inefficiency Argument

To lay the groundwork for my own theory of poverty, I want to delve more deeply into the conventional argument that the poverty-prolonging and poverty-worsening conduct of the poor is inefficient. As the reader will recall from chapter 3, the inefficiency argument assumes that the less of a good one consumes, the greater the satisfaction one gets from a little bit of it. From this premise it is inferred that for those who have very little, additional goods — and the effort needed to get them — should be especially valuable. From the same premise it is also inferred that smoothing consumption over time wrings more satisfaction from a given amount of a good than allowing consumption to vary. For peaks of consumption must add less satisfaction to the satisfaction of average consumption than the corresponding valleys subtract. All this supports the conclusion that poor people who do not work, do not finish school, do not save, do not drink moderately, and do not obey the law waste part of the satisfaction they could derive from their time, energy, money, and other resources.

The argument is persuasive. Its key propositions — that goods and hence work are especially valuable to the poor and that consumption smoothing is efficient for all — will strike many readers as commonsensical. But as widely accepted as these ideas may be in our own day, they are neither obvious nor irresistible once entertained. That they are not obvious is shown by the fact that they have a history. Despite the fact that people have theorized about efficient allocation for millennia, the theory in which these particular ideas are embedded, known as marginalism, dawned on human beings gradually and late, in fact, not until the nineteenth century. The theory took hold among economists slowly in the latter part of the nineteenth century and at the beginning of the twentieth. Only during the twentieth century was it widely disseminated, reaching millions of economics students through economics textbooks, and only in the second half of the twentieth century did it achieve the coveted status of "common sense."[1]

By recounting this history, I shall at the same time introduce the version of the theory that appears in introductory economics textbooks. The version summarized in the paragraph before last can be thought of as the commonsense shadow of the textbook version — faithful in outline but flatter and simpler. Once the assumptions and logic of the textbook version have been made explicit, I will be ready to rebut the theory and suggest something better. Those with a good understanding of introductory microeconomics may want to skip directly to this rebuttal, which is in chapter 5.

The Law of Diminishing Marginal Utility

The foundation of marginalism is the law of diminishing marginal utility of consumption. This is the great principle I expressed informally by saying that the less of a good one consumes, the greater the satisfaction one derives from a little bit of it. The name of the formal principle includes two key terms — "marginal" and "utility." "Marginal" literally means "at the edge," and "utility" is a piece of nineteenth-century philosophical jargon that covers both positive experience and relief — though the so-called utilitarians largely overlooked the difference between those two things. Thus the law literally says that as consumption increases by equal amounts, the additions to the consumer's positive experience or relief that are produced by these increases get smaller and smaller. In other words, while the amount of positive experience or relief that a consumer gets from a good (money, food) grows as consumption grows, the positive experience or relief grows slower than the consumption.[2]

The English philosopher and social thinker Jeremy Bentham (1748–1832) clarified the law of diminishing marginal utility with an example worth quoting because it resonates with common experience (as rebuttals have rarely succeeded in doing): "The matter of wealth is of no value, but in proportion to its influence in respect of happiness. Multiply the sum of a man's property by 2, by 10, by 100, by 1000, there is not the smallest reason for supposing that the sum of his happiness is increased by any such proportion, or in any one approaching to it: multiply his property by a thousand, it may still be a matter of doubt, whether, by that vast addition, you add as much to his happiness as you take away from it by dividing his property by 2, by taking from him but the half of it."[3]

Interestingly, the idea of diminishing marginal utility itself does not crop up explicitly until the eighteenth century. It was spelled out for the first time in 1738 by the Swiss mathematician Daniel Bernoulli.[4] Bernoulli inferred the so-called law from the fact that people were generally averse to risk. According to him, the reason that people with ten dollars will generally decline to bet five of them double-or-nothing on the toss of a coin is that the difference in the satisfaction derived from five dollars and the satisfaction derived from ten is bigger than the satisfaction difference between ten dollars and fifteen. Someone contemplating such a bet stands to gain and lose the same sum of money, but the satisfaction the person stands to gain is less than the satisfaction the person stands to lose. The economic historian George Stigler notes that this argument for the law was buttressed later by the work of the psychologists Ernst Weber and Gustav Fechner, whose experiments showed that physical stimuli in general produce diminishing marginal sensation. Twice the weight does not feel twice as heavy, twice the noise does not sound twice as loud, and so forth.[5]

If we are to judge by the way the law is supported in modern economics textbooks, however, the best case for the law of diminishing marginal utility is neither risk-aversion nor psychophysics It is direct experience. Do we not just *know* from introspection that the extra quantities of pleasure we get from consuming more units of a good grow smaller and smaller? The phenomenon of satiation seems to be an inescapable reality of our inner lives, a reality whose existence does not have to be proved with evidence. Accordingly, textbook after textbook does not so much argue for the law as simply remind young readers of what they already know, that the second soda or hamburger or movie or trip to Europe in a short period is not as satisfying as the first, and the third is not as satisfying as the second, and so forth.[6] Anyone proposing to challenge the law of diminishing marginal utility must explain why this common experience fails to prove it.

From the Law of Diminishing Marginal Utility to the Rule of Equimarginal Allocation

Here, then, is the law of diminishing marginal utility, on which the marginalists' approach to resource allocation rests — and in turn the notion that poor people often allocate inefficiently. The first person to see the logical implications of diminishing marginal utility for allocation was H. H. Gossen. The eccentric Prussian published his groundbreaking piece of reasoning in 1854, and it is found in virtually all introductory economics texts today.[7] To start with Gossen's conclusion, what the marginalist rule of allocation says is that the total benefit of a resource is maximized when the benefits of the last bits of the resource that are devoted to each competing use are equal. In allocating a good between rival uses or occasions, then, we should split it in such a way that the benefit of the last bit of the good that is given to use A is the same as the benefit of the last bit of the good that is given to use B, and so on. This is sometimes called the rule of equimarginal allocation and sometimes, a little tendentiously, the rational allocation rule. It is important to note that marginalists regard the rule of equimarginal allocation as an all-but-universal test of rational allocation.[8] For instance, marginalists treat their rule as working equally well for the allocation of pleasure-giving and misery-relieving amounts of resources, though this is less an explicit doctrine than a consequence of their overlooking the difference between positive experience and relief. (I will argue later that the conflation of positive experience and relief is utterly fatal to the marginalist theory of allocation.)

The case for allocating equimarginally is not exactly self-evident. But it can be easily explained, and few people who have made the effort to grasp it have been unpersuaded. It has seemed compelling to probably millions of economics students over the 150 years since it was first stated. Starting with the so-called law of diminishing marginal utility, then, modern thinkers about allocation reasoned their way to the rule of equimarginal allocation as follows.[9] Suppose you find yourself with a resource and two rival (and unrelated) uses. For instance, suppose you find yourself with a dime that could be spent on either penny candies or penny postcards. Obviously as you transferred your pennies from one use to the other, say, from postcards to candies, the satisfaction you would get from candies would go up and the satisfaction you would get from postcards would go down. So far, so good. But recalling that both candies and postcards produce diminishing marginal utility, the best split of the dime *must be* where the satisfaction from the last penny spent on candies is the same as the satisfaction from the last penny spent on postcards. This is the equimarginal split point, the point where the marginal bits of the resource devoted to each use yield equal satisfaction, and it is this point that gives the modern rule its name. Why must this be the best split point? Well, suppose you as the allocator went further. Suppose you went beyond this equal-satisfaction split, whatever it happened to be, and favored candies with an extra penny while disfavoring postcards with one penny fewer. Given diminishing marginal utility, the added satisfaction produced by the extra candy would be *less* than the satisfaction from the previous, equal-satisfaction penny devoted to candy, while the lost satisfaction from postcards would be *more* than the satisfaction from the equal-satisfaction penny spent on postcards. So the satisfaction that would be gained by moving the split point must be less than the satisfaction that would be lost. The same holds for deviating from the equal-satisfaction point in the other direction, favoring postcards with an extra penny. Moreover, the net loss in satisfaction grows with the size of the deviation from the equal-satisfaction split point.

Simplicity of Using the Rule

A great selling point of the rule of equimarginal allocation is that we do not need to feed in a lot of information to get very exact recommendations out of it. All we have to know is whether, for each way of splitting the budgeted resource between use A and use B (etc.), the individual's marginal utility from use A is greater than, equal to, or less than the individual's utility from use B (etc.). For instance, if Jim splits the dime in half, we need to be able to tell whether the utility he gets from the fifth candy is more than, the same as, or less than the utility he gets from the fifth postcard — and so on for all the possible ways of splitting his dime. If the utility from the last unit of the resource devoted to A is greater than the utility of the last unit devoted to B at a given split point, then more of the resource should be devoted to A, so that the marginal utility of the resource in use A falls and the marginal utility of the resource in use B rises. Eventually, as resources are transferred from B to A, the marginal utilities will be the same. Overall utility from the resource will be maximized at that point. Or so claims the rule of equimarginality.

Parenthetically, a behavioral sign that equimarginality has been reached is that the allocator seems indifferent as to whether a proposed budget cut hits use A or use B. The interpersonal application of this rule of thumb is fairly obvious, too, though one needs to assume that similar reactions signal similar feelings: a distribution will be equimarginal when the rival users react the same way to the prospect of a cut in their allocation. Budget officers of large organizations are sometimes accused of being craven bureaucrats for refusing to shift resources between departments when the squawks of the losers are likely to be just as loud as the jubilations of the gainers. Another interpretation is that they have learned to recognize the signs of an equimarginal allocation.

Note that marginalists generalize the reasoning just explained in two significant ways. First, the basic reasoning is commonly applied not only to the problem of allocating between simultaneous uses of a good by someone (Jim's devoting pennies to postcards or candies), but also to the problem of allocating a good between uses by someone at different times (the grasshopper's allocation of corn between summer consumption and winter consumption). What the equimarginal criterion implies in that context is that the grasshopper should keep transferring kernels of corn from its summer surplus to its store for the winter just until the last kernel of corn to be eaten in summer will produce the same amount of pleasure or relief as the last kernel to be consumed in the winter. Second, the rule of equimarginal allocation is also commonly applied to the problem of distribution, in which the rival uses are rival *users*. (Distribution is considered in chapter 8.)

In all its applications, to summarize, the rule entails that the allocator should allocate to each of the rival uses, however many these uses are, in such a way that the last bit of the good devoted to each use yields the same utility as the last bit devoted to every other use.[10]

Before proceeding, I want to pause for a moment to reflect on the achievement of the marginalists. The philosopher Daniel Dennett has suggested that Charles Darwin's theory of natural selection is "the best single idea that anybody has ever had."[11] But if Darwinism transformed human beings' understanding of the world and their place in it, marginalism transformed the world itself. It did so by supporting two broadly inconsistent political doctrines: the laissez-faire doctrine that helping people harms their motivation to help themselves (by reducing the marginal utility of earned income), and the liberal doctrine that governments can increase the general welfare by transferring resources from the rich to the poor (since poor people derive more utility from the transferred resources). The tension between these two progeny of marginalism has helped define world politics for the past century. For giving rise to this history-shaping dilemma and for sheer ingenuity, one might therefore consider marginalism a strong contender for Dennett's interesting honor. But in the end, I do not think it is. For, as I will try to persuade you in the next chapter, marginalism is mistaken.

The Rule and the Poverty-Linked Behaviors

Coming back to the poverty-prolonging/worsening behavior disproportionately engaged in by the poor, the rule of equimarginal allocation evidently implies that such behavior wastes satisfaction. The person who does not work for pay, for instance, apparently derives less satisfaction from his last weekly hour of nonwork activity than he would have derived from that hour if he had spent it working and earning. For the marginal utility of that first hour of work would be very high, owing to the high marginal utility of dollars to the poor; whereas the marginal utility of the fortieth hour that is devoted each week to the alternative activity is presumably low, coming as it does on the heels of the other thirty-nine. The nonworker should therefore stop using that fortieth hour for the nonwork activity and work for that hour instead. Successive transfers of hours from one category to the other will narrow the gap between the marginal utilities of the last hours devoted to the two activities, because the marginal utility of work will fall and the marginal utility of the other activity will rise. Eventually the transfers will result in the equalization of the utilities of the last hours devoted to each activity. At that point the total satisfaction derived from the available hours will be at a maximum. But satisfaction is being wasted as things stand. Similar arguments hold for quitting school and drinking that interferes with normal earning.

As for not saving and crime, evidently the marginalist test implies that the resulting uneven consumption wastes satisfaction too. For instance, the grasshopper in the fable, who does not save, stands to get much less satisfaction from his last kernel of summer corn than he would have gotten from that kernel if it had been his first in the winter. This logic exposes poor people (and nonpoor people) who fail to save, and who commit crimes, to the charge of satisfaction-inefficiency — absent collateral factors like limited opportunity to save. By leveling consumption across periods they would achieve equimarginality and wring the maximum of satisfaction from any given total of goods.

APPENDIX
Using Indifference Curves to Identify Utility-Maximizing Allocations

On a somewhat technical note, many economists would distinguish the marginalists' rule of equimarginal allocation from the twentieth-century behaviorist rule that recommends allocating in such a way that the consumer's budget line is just tangent to the highest indifference curve that the budget line touches. This is not a deep distinction. Taking the case of allocation between two unrelated goods, the marginalists' quest for the equimarginal point and the behaviorists' quest for the point of tangency between the budget line and the highest indifference curve are the same thing by different names. For suppose we calibrate the axes in terms of the underlying good being allocated, for instance, in dollars rather than hats versus shoes. Then the budget line will have a slope of -1. Then the point of tangency occurs where the function that represents the marginal rate of substitution also has a slope of -1, and (assuming behavioral indifference reflects equality of satisfaction) that *is* the equimarginal point.

In addition, the marginalists and the behaviorists make the same assumptions. In particular, neither assumes the full cardinalization of utility (contrary to what is sometimes said about the marginalist approach), and both presuppose that the marginal utility of consumption is diminishing (contrary to what is sometimes said about the behaviorist approach). Marginalism assumes the law of diminishing marginal utility explicitly. Behaviorist economics assumes it implicitly, in asserting that "well-behaved" indifference curves are convex, that is, bowed toward the origin. For what else, besides the law of diminishing marginal utility, can be the basis of the belief that well-behaved indifference curves are convex? It is certainly not a belief that is directly confirmed by the observation of human behavior. After all, many of the observed allocations of poor people (for example, their lopsided allocations of income among distinct time-slices of themselves) suggest that their indifference curves are bowed away from the origin, not toward it.

Often, behavioristic economists try to defend the idea that well-behaved indifference curves are inwardly bowed from behavioral evidence to the contrary by hypothesizing exceptional, behavior-distorting circumstances (for example, for failure to smooth consumption, the lack of saving vehicles). In effect they are arguing that it only *seems* that poor people's indifference curves are normally outwardly bowed because we do not take into account these behavior-distorting conditions. But why do behavioristic economists want to resist the possibility that outwardly bowed curves are normal in the first place? This seems to be due to their underlying conviction that the marginal utility of goods is diminishing. Regardless of poor people's behavior, the thinking goes, rational allocators will "normally" strive to smooth consumption because ("as we all know") equalizing transfers from one time-slice of themselves to another subtract less utility from the first time-slice than they add to the second, receiving time-slice. Granted, most advanced microeconomics texts do not acknowledge any such underlying assumption of the law of diminishing marginal utility. But this leaves the supposed normality of convex indifference curves with no foundation at all. Interestingly, at least one advanced text does acknowledge that the convexity hypothesis rests on the law of diminishing marginal utility.[12] Given the similarity of the marginalist and the behaviorist approaches, I have not treated the behaviorist approach separately in this book.

5

A New Way to Rationalize the Conduct that Prolongs and Worsens Poverty

The old man also explains cave medicine as practiced by a "top doctor" who specialized in relieving pain. If you had a pain in your chest, for example, he would put some horribly stinging, burning substance on it, so the much worse pain on the outside would take your mind off the pain on the inside. But then how did he get rid of the new pain? Reiner reasonably asks. "He took a big rock and smashed your foot," says Brooks. And then? "That pain would be relieved when he stuck a twig in your eye." He was "brilliant," the old man confides to Reiner, but I decided I didn't need such a specialist.
— Paraphrase of a Mel Brooks and Carl Reiner "2000-Year-Old-Man" routine, in Meg Greenfield, "The Stick in the Eye," *Washington Post*, June 22, 1998

Marginalism is the conventional wisdom about satisfaction-efficient allocation. At its core is the idea that resources mean most to those who have least. On this basis it is natural to conclude that poor people stand to benefit especially from working for pay, staying in school, and moderating alcohol consumption; and that, like everybody else, they stand to benefit from saving for a rainy day and living within the law. Thus marginalism appears to mean that the failures of the poor to do these things are wastes of satisfaction. Since no rational person would throw away satisfaction, marginalism seems therefore to support dysfunctionalism—the view that blames poverty-prolonging and poverty-worsening behaviors on psychological dysfunctions of the poor.

But conventional *opposition* to dysfunctionalism presupposes marginalism too. Marginalism is the starting point of efforts to rationalize poverty by arguing that the dysfunctionality of poor people is an illusion caused by neglecting the restrictedness of their opportunities, or by neglecting the atypicality of their preferences, or by neglecting bad public policy. In short, conventional theories of poverty are divided into those that assert that the conduct in question really contravenes marginalist prescriptions and those that contend the contravening is a mirage—but neither side questions the validity of marginalism itself.

I want to contend that both sides in this conventional debate are making a mistake by accepting marginalist criteria of efficiency in the first place. The reformers are in the middle of the wrong debate about poverty. Instead of talking about whether the conduct does or does not meet the usual criteria of efficiency, they should be asking whether the usual criteria are the right criteria. In this chapter, I will try to persuade you that marginalism itself is mistaken by presenting reasons to doubt its ultimate premise, the law of diminishing marginal utility—and reasons to accept an alternative. On this basis I will give a new argument for the efficiency of the poverty-linked conduct in question.

Lydian Prudence—and Its Premise

We saw in the previous chapter that marginalism is not so obvious that people have believed it all along. It has a history. But is marginalism one of those theories that everybody sees is true the moment they consider it? Certainly the textbooks of today treat it as very nearly irresistible, devoting much more space to explaining it than to proving it. But to help loosen its grip on you, I ask you to consider the following passage from Herodotus's *Histories*. In it the fifth-century B.C. historian describes the practices adopted by the Lydian people of Asia Minor in the face of a prolonged famine:

> Apart from the fact that they prostitute their daughters, the Lydian way of life is not unlike our own. The Lydians were the first people we know of to use a gold and silver coinage and to introduce retail trade, and they also claim to have invented the games which are now commonly played both by themselves and by the Greeks. These games are supposed to have been invented at the time when they sent a colony to settle in Tyrrhenia, and the story is that in the reign of Atys, the son of Manes, the whole of Lydia suffered from a severe famine. For a time the people lingered on as patiently as they could, but later, when there was no improvement, they began to look for something to alleviate their misery. Various expedients were devised: for instance, the invention of dice, knuckle-bones, and ball-games. In fact they claim to have invented all games of this sort except draughts. The way they used these inventions to help them endure their hunger was to eat and play on alternative days — one day playing so continuously that they had no time to think of food, and eating on the next without playing at all.

They managed to live like this for eighteen years. There was still no remission of their suffering — indeed it grew worse; so the King divided the population into two groups and determined by drawing lots which should emigrate and which should remain at home. He appointed himself to rule the section whose lot determined that they should remain, and his son Tyrrhenus to command the emigrants. The lots were drawn, and one section went down to the coast at Smyrna, where they built vessels, put aboard all their household effects, and sailed in search of a livelihood elsewhere. They passed many countries and finally reached Umbria in the north of Italy where they settled and still live to this day.[1]

What is significant here? To begin with, like many poor people today, the Lydians allocated their meager resources unevenly between time-slices of themselves. If we assume that "severe famine" means a condition in which luxurious consumption cannot be achieved even by saving, their pattern must have been "skimp a little / skimp a lot": eat no more than enough one day and nothing the next. Further indication of their preference for uneven consumption is the very fact that what they used to distract themselves from hunger was games of dice and similar games. Assuming they gambled on these games and that they staked their meager holdings, the result for the individual would have been further oscillation in consumption, over and above the practice of eating on alternate days.

While uneven consumption is inefficient when judged by modern criteria of economic efficiency, Herodotus's passage gives us reason to wonder whether the Lydians were not being prudent and sensible after all. For one thing, their practices resulted from careful thought about how to minimize misery. Impulse, apathy, and indifference to the future are not even hinted at. Moreover, the passage suggests that the Lydians' strategy was sophisticated as well as deliberate, for they are described as being the inventors of not only gold and silver coinage but retailing. Third, the practices continued for eighteen years, surely enough time for the Lydians to compare the results with those of smoothing consumption over time. Nor does Herodotus present the practices as efficient only in the sense that they satisfied unusual enthusiasms, such as a preference for variety per se or an addiction to the excitement of gambling. For he makes the point early on that the Lydians are not atypical: "Their way of life is not unlike our own."

In short, this passage indicates that at least one society in the distant past adopted countermarginalist patterns on the basis of smart, careful thinking, and that it stuck to them in the light of long experience, for reasons having nothing to do with atypical preferences.

What assumption might the Lydians have made that would explain their seeing these patterns of consumption as efficient? One possibility is that they assumed the marginal utility of resources at truly insufficient levels of consumption is increasing instead of diminishing. In other words, when there is not enough of a good, equal increases in consumption bring bigger and bigger amounts of relief. Such an assumption is contrary, of course, to the law of diminishing marginal utility, which hypothesizes diminishing marginal utility at low levels of consumption as well as high. But suppose the Lydians were assuming exactly this. It would follow that the benefit of a meager portion is more than twice the benefit of half of it. Therefore eating half as much every day as the Lydians were in fact eating every other day — which is to say, smoothing consumption — would actually have *wasted* potential benefit from the food supply. Imputing this assumption to the Lydians makes sense of the pattern they actually adopted.

Furthermore, if marginal utility is increasing at low levels of consumption, then typical people whose consumption is very low will derive very little utility from a bit more consumption. This makes sense of another part of the story. Like many poor people in modern times, it seems that the famine-oppressed Lydians did little work. Rather, they played games "continuously" every other day. We are not told why they did little work. It may have been that farming, fishing, and hunting were simply not worth the effort because of the stinginess of nature in that time and place. But there is another possibility. If marginal utility is increasing amid true scarcity, then perhaps they did little work because — having very little food, for whatever reason — marginal increases in their diet were worth little to them, contrary though this idea may be to the law of diminishing marginal utility and contemporary common sense.

Further, by imputing this assumption to the Lydians, we can make sense of yet another part of the story. Herodotus says that half of the population departed in search of new land and livelihood. This was a risk. Things could have turned out better or worse for anyone leaving. Maybe, in the absence of information, they guessed that the chances of conditions getting better by x or worse by x were equal. Had they made the assumption we imputed to them, that the benefits of insufficient consumption grow faster than consumption, they might have sensibly concluded that the value of taking the risk was greater than the value of staying where they were, since they had more to gain than they had to lose. Algebraically, the utility of the bet $[= \{U \text{ of (status quo} + x)X .5\} + \{U \text{ of (status quo} - x)X .5\}]$ was greater than the utility of the status quo. Adding to the wisdom of that choice from the standpoint of the whole group was the fact that the departure of half left the other half better off.

Now suppose we grant the possibility that a law of increasing marginal utility amid scarcity would make sense of the practices of the Lydians and, to anticipate, of the practices of the poor today. This gives us a reason to believe in increasing marginal utility amid scarcity. But it does not prove it, because the assumption that their conduct *does* make sense is not unassailable, and anyway there are other ways to make sense of the conduct. So we must still ask, *does* the marginal utility of consumption rise when goods are truly scarce? Or is human psychology better captured by the law of diminishing marginal utility, which would have it that even amid scarcity a bit of a good is more satisfying when it is one of few bits than when it is one of many? You may be scratching your head at the very idea of increasing marginal utility, so irresistible has the law of diminishing marginal utility come to seem. But let us look more closely.

Replacing the Law of Diminishing Marginal Utility

I begin by distinguishing three types of goods: relievers, pleasers, and goods that function as relievers at low levels of consumption and pleasers at high levels of consumption.

Relievers

Relievers, such as salves, are goods that reduce pain, unhappiness, or misery. Contrary to the law of diminishing marginal utility, which purports to hold for goods generally, relievers are a major type of good that exhibits increasing (not diminishing) marginal benefit. The benefit of relievers — namely, relief — grows as consumption grows, but the benefit grows faster than the consumption. Equal increases in the consumption of relievers produce ever-bigger increases in the relief that is felt by the consumer.

The best evidence of this is common experience. Consider the following scenarios. In Scenario One, you are sitting quietly in a field and are suddenly stung by a bee on your hand. The spot that was stung hurts terribly, and it is virtually impossible not to pay close attention to it. In Scenario Two, likewise, you are stung on the hand, but at the same moment you also are stung six times elsewhere on your body. Surely the sting on the hand would be much more noticed in the first case, in which it was the only sting, than in the second, in which it was one of seven.[2] The sting on the hand would be like a shout that is striking in a quiet street but hardly noticed in a riot.[3]

Given all this, consider the impact of dabs of salve, each of which we may imagine relieves just one sting. Go back to Scenario Two, the one in which you suffer seven stings. Suppose that in this situation a single dab of salve is applied to the sting on your hand one second after it happens. Bearing in mind that you still have six uncured stings elsewhere on your body, you would not expect applying this one dab to make much difference. It would be like *quieting* one shout in a riot. Most people would pay little for a dab of salve for their hand in this situation. But now change the supposition a bit more. What if, just before the dab is applied to your hand, six dabs of salve are applied to the six stings on your body? This surely makes the impact of the dab of salve on the hand much greater. After all, now the dab on your hand makes the difference between having one uncured sting and having none, which is a much bigger difference than having seven uncured stings and having six. Applying the dab in this case would be like quieting a single shout *in an otherwise quiet street*. Doubtless you would pay much more for a single dab in this situation than in the other. As for the dabs between the first and the seventh, if the marginal misery produced by stings is diminishing, then the marginal relief produced by dabs of salve must be increasing.

Having marginal benefit that increases is not a peculiarity of relievers of physical pain. For one thing, relievers of physical discomforts that are not pains seem to have increasing marginal benefit too. The bee sting story is surely just as plausible for patches of poison ivy on the skin and dabs of calamine lotion.

Further, increasing marginal benefit is not peculiar to cases in which the physical discomfort and its relievers are particulate or discontinuous, as with stings/dabs of salve and itchy patches/dabs of lotion. In fact, the only special significance of the particulate cases, for our purposes, is that the increasing marginal utility of relievers is most easily seen where the bad thing being relieved is particulate. But it can be seen where the bad thing is continuous too. Take the case of burdens — not in the metaphorical sense but in the literal sense of heavy things to be hefted and carried. Here both the negative thing, the weight, and any relieving factor that may lighten the burden can vary continuously. They are not inherently chunky or lumpy. What then is the marginal benefit of relievers such as help in bearing the burden? In fact it is increasing. To clarify this, let us imagine two new scenarios. In the first, you are about to walk up a hill empty-handed when you are given 5 pounds of grain to take with you. The second scenario is identical to the first, except that just before you are given the 5 pounds of grain to carry, you are given 50 pounds of grain to carry. In other words, the contents of a 5-pound sack are simply added to a 50-pound sack. There can be little doubt that in the second scenario, the 5 pounds would seem less burdensome than they would seem in the first scenario. In fact, you might barely notice those 5 pounds on top of the 50 pounds you are already obliged to carry in this scenario. Probably you would not pay much to have a helper carry just those 5 pounds for you, since you would still have to deal with the 50-pound burden. But if all but 6 of the 50 pounds were taken off your hands unexpectedly, being relieved of the 5 pounds would be a greater benefit, since that would make the difference between a 6-pound burden and a 1-pound burden. You would likely pay more to have a helper carry the 5 pounds in this case. As this suggests, the benefit of a certain amount of help in bearing a burden is greater when the burden is less. From here it is a short step to recognizing that successive equal lightenings will bring increasing amounts of subjective relief.

In this case, common experience is confirmed by science. In 1834 Ernst Weber established experimentally that a greater absolute change in a stimulus is required to produce a just noticeable difference in our sensory experience when the stimulus is larger to begin with. Further, Weber showed that for each type of stimulus, the percentage change in the stimulus that is required to produce a subjectively perceptible change is a constant fraction.[4] Coming back to burdens, for a difference in weight to be just noticed, Weber found that there must be a 2 percent change, regardless of whether the object in question is light or heavy. This means, for instance, that subtracting 1 pound from the weight of a 51-pound bag of grain will not make it feel any lighter — 1 being less than 2 percent of 51 — but subtracting a second pound will. If the 51-pound bag is a burden that has to be carried up a hill, then relieving the carrier's burden by a second pound will bring increasing subjective relief at this point — from none to some. Someone who had to carry a 51-pound bag should pay nothing to have a helper carry a first pound of grain for him, but something to have that helper carry a second pound.

What is more, if Weber is correct, each successive just noticeable atom of subjective relief will require less lightening of the sack than the just noticeable atom of relief before it. So while an even pound must be subtracted from the 50-pound sack to make it feel lighter, only 0.98

pound must be subtracted from the 49-pound sack to make it feel lighter, that is, 2 percent of 49; and only a little more than 0.96 pound must be subtracted from the weight that then remains (48.02 pounds) to make *it* feel lighter; and so on. But to say that equal atoms of felt relief require smaller and smaller lightenings of the sack comes very close to saying that equal lightenings will produce bigger and bigger amounts of felt relief. To this extent there is scientific support for the hypothesis of increasing marginal utility amid misery as well as support from common experience. Assuming that the helper charges by weight, the value of marginal dollars spent on relief will be increasing.

Moving now from physical to mental relief, we see the same principle in operation. The first scratch sustained by a new car distresses its owner. It is hard to look at the scratch. Each subsequent scratch causes new displeasure, but as the scratches mount up, the new ones add less and less new distress. The seventh may elicit nothing more than an irritated shrug. So the relief that comes from repairing the very first scratch that the car sustained will be greater if the other six are also being fixed than if the other six are not.

To turn to a different kind of mental discomfort, paying the first bill in a stack of overdue bills does little to relieve a guilty conscience. Having nine overdue bills is only a little less uncomfortable than having ten. But paying the last bill in the stack and moving from one to none is normally a big load off one's mind. That the marginal relief provided by each check written starts small and grows probably accounts for the difficulty of sitting down to do the first one and for the momentum that seems to build as one works one's way to the bottom of the pile. The same increasing marginal benefit seems to explain the low motivation we feel as we approach a sinkful of dirty dishes after dinner and the gathering of momentum we feel as we clean our way through — from the hardly noticeable tenth dish to the very welcome last one.

This introspection-based case for the increasing marginal utility of relievers is structurally identical to the orthodox economists' case for the proposition that almost all goods have diminishing marginal utility. Here, for instance, is an already-cited passage from a popular microeconomics textbook: "To see why marginal utility diminishes, think about the following two situations: In one, you've just been studying for 29 evenings. An opportunity arises to see a movie. The utility you get from that movie is the marginal utility from seeing one movie in a month. In the second situation, you've been on a movie binge. For the past 29 nights, you have not even seen an assignment. You are up to your eyeballs in movies. You are happy enough to go to a movie on yet one more night. But the thrill that you get out of that thirtieth movie in 30 days is not very large. It is the marginal utility of the thirtieth movie in a month."[5]

To see the structural identity, all we have to do is imagine that the affective charge of movies for the consumer is flipped from positive to negative. That is, imagine that the reader addressed by the passage dislikes movies instead of liking them, but she finds herself in a college course that requires her to see a movie every evening for a solid month. The first night is doubtless hard to bear, but by night thirty, the student will be saying things like, "Well, what's one more unpleasant evening on top of all those others?"[6] Accordingly, a reliever such as a waiver from her teacher that exempts her from the thirtieth movie will be worth relatively little to her, while waivers that exempted her from movies earlier in the inurement process would have been worth more. In light of this structural identity, it is hard to see how someone who finds the textbook arguments for the diminishing marginal utility of positive goods convincing could object to our argument for the increasing marginal utility of relievers.

Why does this pattern hold? The human mind can attend to only so much. Inevitably, we have to exclude from awareness some of what is presented to us. This can be done by keeping objects out of conscious awareness altogether, as when the rapt reader fails to notice the doorbell.[7] Or it can be done by diminishing the impression that individual objects make upon us, without excluding the objects in their entirety. It is this diminishment function of attention that we see operating with the stings, itches, burdens, paint scratches, unpaid bills, and unwashed dishes. Significantly, the more items are presented, the more diluted is the impression made by each. Conversely, relievers intensify awareness of each evil left uncanceled. It is for just this reason, namely, that they obliterate ever more striking causes of misery, that relievers bring progressively more benefit.[8]

Pleasers

These are goods that cause positive experience, as distinct from removing negative experience. Examples might include a glass of wine along with a meal or a portion of ice cream at the end. To lose a pleaser or not to have one is not an evil but only the undoing or absence of a good. Interestingly, while the word "reliever" is a natural name for things that undo the effect of evils, there does not seem to be a name for things that obliterate the effect of pleasers, other than "killjoys," perhaps.

Unlike relievers, pleasers *do* generally conform to the law of diminishing marginal utility. That is because what the limits of human attention are diminishing in this case is objects with a positive charge. Virtually all introductory economics textbooks remind students of the psychological impact of successive pleasers that are familiar from everyday experience, things like desserts and movies, to win support for the law of diminishing marginal utility. Students readily agree that the third helping of dessert brings less pleasure than the first, and so forth. But the textbooks do not recognize that significant classes of goods are not pleasers (or not pleasers at all levels of consumption — see below), and so they claim far more generality for the law of diminishing marginal utility than they should.[9]

Reliever/Pleasers

The third class of goods, reliever/pleasers, is the most important for understanding poverty. Reliever/pleasers do not fall completely into either of the preceding categories. Rather, they are relievers at low levels of consumption and pleasers at high levels of consumption. Examples include many basic goods — things that benefit virtually all consumers: food, shelter, clothing, transportation, leisure, and opportunities to take part in community life. Characteristic of these goods, besides being generally valued, is that they can be used or consumed at three levels: insufficient levels, where shortfalls make for misery and more consumption makes for relief; sufficient levels, which cause neither misery nor positive pleasure; and above-sufficient levels, where the consumer takes a positive enjoyment or satisfaction from consuming them.

Again, the set of goods that serve as both pleasers and relievers includes many basic goods. But some basic goods are not reliever/pleasers. Water benefits everyone, but because it does not usually bring positive enjoyment once thirst has been relieved, it is usually a pure reliever. Sex may be a case of a basic good that does not fit for the opposite reason, that while its occurrence brings pleasure, for many people, at least, its absence is not a source of misery.

The "dual citizenship" of goods of this third type shows itself in their marginal benefit. They act just like pure relievers when insufficient amounts are being consumed, which is to say, they yield increasing marginal benefit. But they act just like pure pleasers when more-than-sufficient amounts are being consumed, which is to say, they yield diminishing marginal benefit. The point is a central one in this book. To repeat, the marginal benefit of reliever/pleasers is first rising and then falling. In the insufficient range (where by definition additional quantities bring relief), equal additions to consumption produce bigger and bigger additional benefits, but in the more-than-sufficient range, equal additions produce smaller and smaller additional benefits. For this class of goods, in short, the applicable generalization is not the law of diminishing marginal utility but a *law of diminishing marginal impact of deviations from sufficiency.* This may seem complicated, but on the contrary it is the law of diminishing marginal utility that is complicated. After all, the law of diminishing marginal utility implies that the marginal impact of deficits is rising while the marginal impact of surpluses is falling. Why should that be?

Examples of Basic Goods That Are Reliever/Pleasers, with Increasing Marginal Impact at Low Levels of Consumption

Consider housing. Suppose we take the perspective of a couple whose house has a bedroom for them and one for each of their six children, plus adequate room for entertaining and other functions besides. Clearly they are consuming or using housing in the more-than-sufficient range. Their house is a source of positive experience. As each child leaves for college (let us say), the amount of space available for the use of the couple goes up by roughly equal amounts, but probably their enjoyment of the house goes up by smaller and smaller amounts. To take a small but representative aspect, the new hobbies that can now be pursued because there are specialized spaces for them (sewing, exercise, painting, etc.) will themselves yield smaller and smaller amounts of additional pleasure, if only because the more there are, the less attention can be paid to each one. (We can ignore special discontinuities that might arise, such as the crucial square foot of freed-up space that makes it possible to play indoor tennis.)

But now imagine a couple whose dwelling is a one-bedroom house that is barely adequate for themselves. If a child arrives, then, given the crowded conditions, the couple's privacy is much reduced, their peace and quiet is disturbed, and they may have to start sleeping in shifts. Whatever the compensating joys of parenthood may be, these are impressive deteriorations in their physical comfort. By the time child number six arrives, the couple may hardly notice the further deterioration in their situation that occurs as a result. One more loud voice outside the bedroom door will not make much difference. One more child in one's path as one stumbles to the bathroom at night may not add much misery. Accordingly, as the children grow up and move out, and space per inhabitant goes up, the first child to leave may not subtract much discomfort from the couple's life. After all, if one more voice outside the bedroom door did not add much discomfort, one fewer should not subtract much discomfort either. But when the sixth child finally moves out, undoing the impressive deterioration created by the first baby, the relief may be enormous. This story pulls together reminders of common experience to show that while the marginal benefit of housing space per inhabitant may be diminishing at high levels, it is rising at low levels.

As another example, consider ways of getting from place to place. We need hardly argue that transportation in the more-than-adequate range, where it is a source of pleasure, displays diminishing marginal benefit. Very rich people usually limit their spending on automobiles for this very reason. There is usually something that even billionaires want more than a two-hundred-thousand-dollar car.

But compare transportation in the insufficient range, where the lack is the cause of unhappiness. Let us think of the problem in very concrete terms. Imagine a poor worker who cannot afford even a bus ticket to travel the six miles between her home and her workplace, so she has to walk. As a result, she suffers various kinds of troubles. From the walking itself she develops blisters on her feet. Owing to the pressures on her time, her one-room house gets messy. On account of fatigue, she makes mistakes at work, which elicit reprimands from her employer.

Now suppose that her neighbor offers to drive her one mile of the six-mile journey in exchange for conversing with him in French as they drive. And let's assume, overneatly for the sake of clarity, that the worker's troubles would diminish in proportion to the reduction in her long hike. Instead of six blisters, she would get five. Instead of six unwashed dishes in her sink, there would be only five, since she would have a little more time for cleaning. Since she would be a little less tired, her workplace mistakes would go from six a day to five as well, which would mean one fewer reprimand from her employer. Will she, if rational, take the deal? Of course, it turns on facts not yet specified, like the burdensomeness of speaking French with her neighbor. Maybe the neighbor's French is fairly good, and the chore is a light one, but maybe it is so bad that she finds conversing with him exhausting. Supposing the chore is in fact burdensome, then, given all we have said about the limitations of attention, the worker may well refuse the deal. After all, she may reason, how much difference will it make to be relieved of one blister, one unwashed dish, and one scolding when there are five other blisters, unwashed dishes, and reprimands still to endure? When she is walking all six miles, and there are six instances of each trouble to bear, her attention to each one is diminished by the presence of the others. Each is like a shout in a riot. To relieve just one of each is like quieting a single shout in a riot. She may barely notice the improvement.

But now change the scenario. What if the neighbor starts by giving the worker a five-mile ride, no strings attached, leaving her only a mile to walk? Sticking to our simplification, the worker will now be suffering only one blister, leaving only one dish unwashed, and making only one mistake a day. Because the number is reduced, each of these will command much greater attention than the identical problem received in the previous scenario. The soup bowl in the sink makes a bigger impression on its own than it did as one of six unwashed dishes, and so on. Now suppose that, having made the unconditional gift, the neighbor makes the same offer as before: a one-mile ride in exchange for a little French conversation. Isn't the worker likelier to take the deal in this situation? After all, the chore is the same, but the potential relief is much greater, because the difference between one blister, one unwashed dish, and one reprimand and none will feel much bigger than the difference between six and five. Now the effect of taking the deal will be like quieting a shout in an otherwise quiet street.

Blisters, dishes, and reprimands, of course, are neither here nor there. The point is that equal improvements in transportation that relieve equal troubles will have increasing subjective impact. From here it is a short step to the conclusion that the marginal utility of transportation dollars for the poor worker is increasing: the dollar that buys her a one-mile ride has a greater marginal utility — not a lesser marginal utility, as conventional wisdom would have it — when that dollar is combined with enough dollars to buy her a ride for the other five miles.

As a third example, consider leisure as contrasted with work in the broad sense of the term: time not spent working for pay, volunteering, at a serious avocation, etc. Such leisure can be insufficient, sufficient, or more than enough. When there is more than enough of it, additional hours add progressively less and less pleasure. This is because the limits of attention increasingly diminish the impression made by the pleasant things that fill each hour. The tenth day in a row of fishing, social conversation, beach reading, and golf will make a fainter positive impact than the first.

But compare the impact of increased leisure in the insufficient range. Again, we will do well to look at the issue concretely. People who work too much tend to find their hours on the job oppressive. And besides the burden of what they are doing, there is the burden of what they are not doing, which is to say, the disappointment they feel on account of missing the anniversary, the school play, the big game, the regular weekend golf match, along with the resentment of the family members and friends they have neglected. Both the burden of commission and the burdens of omission grow as leisure time shrinks, of course. But the notable point for our purposes is that the extra misery produced by one more hour at the desk, and the extra disappointment and resentment produced by missing one more anniversary, school play, or golf game tend to become less and less as the totals mount. As the absolute losses accumulate, the individual case gets less and less attention. Eventually, for instance, children become inured to the no-shows of a workaholic parent, and the parent for his part becomes inured to the resentment that does come his way. Assuming the extra income earned from the last few hours of work has a relatively high marginal utility, so-called workaholic behavior will be rational for such a person at the margin. More is to be lost than gained from a modest cutback in work hours.

Conversely, the felt relief from increased leisure will grow progressively. Leisure hours for the person with insufficient leisure are like salve. For instance if "time on task" falls from seventy hours a week to sixty, the relief at work and at home will be relatively minor, in keeping with the fact that the marginal distress produced by those ten hours was small. But when the work week goes from fifty hours to forty, say, the relief will be larger, since the no-shows, instances of neglect, and so on that are being eliminated now have not been competing for attention with so many others and thus make a less diminished impression. All of this may be summarized by saying that the marginal benefit of hours of leisure is rising up to the point where leisure is no longer insufficient, and only then, when there is more than enough, does the marginal benefit start to diminish.

In practical terms, the hypothesis also suggests that the best strategy for the neglected spouse of the "rational workaholic" may be simply demanding a cut in his or her work hours. Since having more leisure should raise the workaholic's appreciation of marginal hours of leisure, the chances of the person's taking *further* time off may rise, depending, of course, on how much utility stands to be lost from the income reduction that goes with working less.

As a last illustration, consider opportunities to participate politically and socially in community life. To be clear, I am not talking here about major outrages such as being deprived of due process of law, but about the large array of slights, exclusions, and petty insults that members of minority groups have notoriously suffered even in recent decades. The sting of being deprived of a particular opportunity resembles a physical sting in at least this way: it is likely to be less keenly felt when one is inured to it by many others. Witness the sad fact that victims of discrimination often just shrug at one more slight. Predictably, they may not get much relief from a single opportunity to participate or show much appreciation for it. But when most kinds of opportunity have already been extended, and only a few gaps remain, alleviating one more objectively equal slight makes a bigger difference, like extinguishing a single torch against the night sky. This may help explain the curious fact that it has usually been the less oppressed among the oppressed, and not the truly wretched, who have pushed hardest for political and social change, contrary to the predictions of Karl Marx. In any case, as the formerly deprived are given more and more opportunities, a point is reached when they no longer feel much deprivation, and they begin to enjoy further opportunities positively. From here on, as this reliever/pleaser good enters its pleasing range, the marginal benefit of each new opportunity begins to grow smaller and smaller. The most privileged people in the community may hardly notice one more invitation to participate.

The reader can doubtless extend this list of basic goods that are reliever/pleasers with increasing marginal benefit at low levels of consumption, but these examples should be enough to suggest the underlying logic: deficits of basic goods bring troubles, and troubles, like other stimuli, have diminishing marginal impact; so basic goods themselves at subsufficient levels have increasing marginal impact.

Toward a Solution of the Puzzles

We can now begin to unravel the puzzles of poverty identified in chapter 3. To remind you, the puzzles of poverty are basically two, one about work and the other about consumption smoothing. First, seeing that poor people stand to gain the most from income and the effort that earns it, why do poor people so often (a) remain outside the workforce, (b) drop out of school, passing up the chance to boost later wages, and (c) drink in quantities that interfere with earning capacity? Second, why do poor people disproportionately fail to save for a rainy day and even introduce wide variation in their consumption by committing crimes, when they, like all of us, stand to gain from smoothing consumption?

One element of the answer is a point that will be recalled from chapter 1. Recall the definitional link between poverty and insufficiency. The poor people in any time and place are those whose consumption does not meet what are considered basic needs in that time and place. Their consumption is insufficient, and they suffer on that account. Hence small improvements in their consumption bring relief of suffering rather than positive satisfaction. A second element of the answer has been proposed and supported in the preceding pages of this chapter: for goods capable of bringing both relief and positive satisfaction, marginal consumption increases in the reliever range cause increasing — rather than diminishing — additions to utility. Having insufficient living space, transportation, leisure, etc. is like having too few dabs of salve for one's stings, in that equal increases of consumption (up to the level of sufficiency) bring increasing amounts of added relief. Putting these pieces together, I suggest that poor people engage disproportionately in the poverty-prolonging and poverty-worsening behaviors *because they are poor* — and rational. For this conduct is exactly the conduct that makes sense for them, given the psychological truth that goods serving as relievers have increasing marginal utility.

To be more specific about nonwork, the postulate of increasing marginal utility makes sense of the fact that very poor people are less likely to exert themselves for money than others. After all, they stand to benefit *less* from a given addition to their income than not-so-poor people do — not more, as conventional wisdom would have it. So at any given wage, they stand to gain less from an hour of paid work. Recall the person with seven bee stings who would not sacrifice much to relieve the sting on his hand, seeing that the pain of it was nearly drowned out by the pain of the six stings on his body. This would seem to be the position of very poor people, for whom work, school-work, and (in a much different way) moderation in alcohol use constitute sacrifices that would buy them too little felt relief to be worth making, so many are their troubles.

To be more specific about consumption smoothing, the postulate of increasing marginal utility amid poverty can also rationalize the fact that poor people are less likely than others to save for a rainy (or rainier) day, because, according to that postulate, leveling income wastes some of the relief that could have been wrung from the sum of the available resources over time. The poor person whose income varies for reasons beyond his control is like someone who awakes every morning with two stings that will hurt all day if not treated with dabs of salve, and who awakes every second day with two dabs of salve on his bedside table. Seeing that two stings are less than twice as painful as one, relieving one is less than half as beneficial as relieving two. So it would be a waste of potential relief to lay aside one dab from the pair he gets on alternate days in order to smooth consumption at the level of one dab per day. At the end of a month, in other words, the same number of dabs will be consumed whether the pattern is 2–0–2–0 . . . or 1–1–1–1 . . . , but the total amount of relief is greater with the first pattern than with the second. In fact, if the total amount of relief gotten from 2–0–2–0 . . . is greater than the total relief from 1–1–1–1 . . . , an efficient allocator will be willing to sacrifice some of his total monthly allotment of dabs in exchange for the option of using the remaining dabs unevenly. As we will see in a moment, this seems to be an important consideration in rationalizing the real-world patterns of poor people with regard to education, saving, and crime.

To clarify the logic of uneven consumption by poor people further, we might turn our attention from salve to a basic good — transportation. Think back to the poor worker who has to walk six miles to work, causing blisters, unwashed dishes in the sink at home, and reprimands from her employer. Now suppose that her employer introduces a new fringe benefit: each month she gets a voucher for a certain number of miles of riding on the bus, and this lets her ride the whole way. But also suppose that for some reason the vouchers are not given for two months out of each year. Should she save her miles so that she can ride five of the six miles all year, or should she ride all the way for ten months out of the year and walk all the way the other two months? Given the increasing marginal utility of miles of transportation in the misery-relieving range, she is better off in the long term not saving but rather riding all the way for ten months. The five-mile ride relieves less than five-sixths as much misery as the six-mile ride. Indeed, the five-mile ride may be barely better than no ride at all. Putting it the other way around, that sixth mile makes for a disproportionate reduction in her misery. So even though the total miles ridden are the same on either plan, the total misery relieved is more on the ten-month plan.

To avert possible confusion, note that the issue here is not saving per se but consumption smoothing. After all, the Lydians did save amid scarcity: they saved their food every other day, so they could eat it on the next. But there is no contradiction in saying that both the poor Lydians who saved and the poor worker who does not save are being efficient, because the Lydians were creating consumption variation by saving, while the poor worker who does not save is thereby preserving consumption variation.

Now as with the dabs, so with the miles of transportation: the rational worker will be willing to sacrifice part of the year's total allotment of miles in exchange for the opportunity to use the remaining miles unevenly. Specifically, the rational worker will be willing to sacrifice any number of miles up to the number that wipes out the utility advantage of uneven consumption. So suppose that her employer decides to introduce a savings plan. This plan gives a few bonus bus miles to those employees who save some of their monthly allotment of miles so as to cover all twelve months at the same level. It is easy to imagine the employer offering this plan. As a member of the middle class (presumably), for whom marginal additions to consumption add positive experiences that get smaller and smaller, he will, of course, be used to the idea that consumption leveling wrings the maximum amount of utility from any good over time. He is likely to regard the offer of bonus miles for saving as just an incentive for employees with short time horizons to come to their senses and do the right thing for themselves. Nevertheless, the employer may be surprised at how few employees sign up for the savings plan. In order to induce participation, the bonus may have to be very — and to him bewilderingly — large because the bonus is not a prod to do what is efficient, as he imagines, but a compensation for doing what would be inefficient without it — namely, spreading the miles out over the whole year. This story sheds light on several patterns that strike observers of the poor.

Saving

As noted in chapter 3, the common failure of poor people to save for a rainy day is doubly puzzling to common sense because it means not only failing to smooth consumption but passing up the chance to increase *total* consumption, given the availability of interest on saved money. But if it is *varying* the level of consumption over time that is satisfaction-efficient for poor people, then we would expect fewer of them than of higher-income people to save for a rainy day at any given level of interest. For the interest payments in their case have to compensate them for doing something that is otherwise inefficient. In other words, they will willingly accept certain sacrifices in total consumption over time in order to be able to consume whatever they consume unevenly.

Illegal Activity

Obviously, people choose whether to engage in illegal activity on the basis of noneconomic considerations as well as economic ones. But the purely economic perspective is revealing nonetheless. The logic that illuminates comparatively low savings rates among the poor, despite the availability of interest, can also illuminate the disproportionate tendency of poor people to engage in illegal activity despite the long-term income sacrifices that are in store for the habitual criminal, as we saw in chapter 2. To begin with, criminal careers cause variations in income, and these, as we know, are generally desirable for the poor. To take a trivial example, a poor person may stand to get more relief over time if he parks illegally each day and incurs a 50 percent risk of getting a $10 ticket than if he pays $5 each day to park legally. For the illegal scheme will tend to mean that the annual cost of parking is paid out unevenly, making for a variation in the amount that remains for relieving amounts of goods other than parking. And such variation will, of course, be welcome. Figuratively, it is better in the long run to cure both of one's daily pair of stings every other day than to cure one of the pair every day. And the utility advantage of consumption variation may be so great that even the utility loss that comes with a reduction of long-term income may not outweigh it. For instance, even if better enforcement raises the chances of getting a ticket to 60 percent, so that the annual cost of parking illegally becomes greater than that of parking legally, the poor person may rationally persist in parking illegally. He may not stop till the odds of getting a ticket rise even higher. Recalling chapter 2, this logic could rationalize the puzzling tendency of some poor people to commit serious property crimes repeatedly, even though they could make more money in the long run at a regular job. To deter them, evidently, the differential in long-term income must somehow be made bigger, or their income must be raised somehow to the level where consumption smoothing is actually efficient.

The reverse holds for nonpoor people, since they are in the income range where marginal utility diminishes and consumption-smoothing wrings the maximum utility from a given income. Figuratively, it is better to enjoy a dessert after every dinner than to enjoy two desserts after dinner every other day. But if so, then only the prospect of a long-term income *advantage* will induce a nonpoor person to give up the smoothness of his usual consumption by engaging in a career of illegal activity. Going back to our trivial example, it will take a fall in the probability of getting a ticket to something less than 50 percent to induce a rational nonpoor person to park illegally; and the utility advantage of smoothing may be so great that the odds of getting a ticket will have to be substantially lower than 50 percent, making the annual cost of illegal parking much lower than that of legal parking, before he will consider adopting that pattern. Since few criminal careers pay middle-class individuals better than regular employment in the long term, it makes sense from a sheer economic perspective that there are few middle-class career criminals.

Educational Persistence

Chapter 3 looked at the seeming paradox of an income-linked difference in educational persistence: if education raises earning power, then shouldn't the poorest people, who have the most to gain from an increase of income, be especially eager to persist? Part of the solution has already been mentioned. Contrary to the premise of the paradox, the poorest people do *not* have the most to gain from an increase in income, and so it is not surprising that they do not especially value the means for increasing income, either direct work or schoolwork that raises later wages. But there is an additional factor. Consider the financial returns on academic effort, on the out-of-pocket costs of education and on the earnings that have to be foregone. These returns normally take the form of wage enhancements. This means that along with wages themselves, the payback on education tends to flow smoothly to the investor. (Compare the payback on training for a career as an athlete.) To the extent that the smoothness of the flow makes it hard to consume the returns unevenly, the appeal of education to the poor will therefore be reduced. For again, level consumption wastes relief. Everything else being equal, then, education will be less appealing to poor people than investments whose returns can be consumed quickly. Only the prospect of significant returns on their time-and-money investment will entice poor people to persist in school, since such returns have to compensate them for accepting what would otherwise be an inefficient pattern of consumption. Extending the same principle to the choice among types of education, we should not be surprised either that poor people often prefer career-phase-specific training — training whose benefits are confined to one period — over education whose benefits extend over whole careers, such as liberal arts education.

If my suggestion is correct, then, poor people are not cool toward education because they are imprudent or because their cultures are hostile to academic success. (This recently popular theory is belied in any case by the reverence for learning that is so obvious in the traditions of the very subcultures with the biggest dropout problems, such as the African American subculture.) Rather, poor people are cool toward education because they are poor — and rational.

Where Does This Solution Leave the Conventional Theories of Poverty?

My proposal is that the poverty-prolonging and poverty-worsening conduct discussed in chapter 2 makes sense for reasons having nothing to do with restricted opportunity, atypical preferences, or perverse public policies. Does this hypothesis mean that the conventional accounts of this behavior are mistaken?

If the three versions of dysfunctionalism (apathy, self-alienation, *akrasia*) are meant to account for the poverty-linked conduct *generally*, it is hard to see what is left of their initial appeal. For the thing they are brought in to explain, the supposed inefficiency of the conduct in general ("Why would poor people shoot themselves in the foot like this?") has turned out to be an illusion. This is not to deny that poor people *sometimes* engage in the poverty-linked conduct because of apathy, short time horizons, and so forth. For instance, a poor individual may try to smooth consumption by saving, mistakenly believing this to be efficient on the basis of bad advice, but then fail to save for lack of self-discipline and wind up varying his consumption anyway — to his benefit. In odd cases like this, of course, dysfunctionality itself will cost the individual nothing, though there is a danger that it may persist after the individual has ceased to be poor, at which point it may become a liability. What I do find implausible is that poor people *usually* engage in the poverty-linked conduct because of apathy, short time horizons, or lack of willpower. It seems a stretch to generalize from a modest number of bona fide cases of, say, nonwork due to depression to explain why millions and millions of poor people do not work. And not only are there too few indisputable examples, there are too many impressive counterexamples — obviously nondepressed nonworkers, in this case. Moreover, parsimony argues against dividing human behavior into the rational and the irrational along income lines. But above all, common experience supports a hypothesis about the relation of income and utility that makes the behavior look efficient rather than inefficient, leaving dysfunctionalism with little to explain.

The question of where my hypothesis leaves the conventional theories of restricted opportunity, atypical preferences, and perverse public policies is a little more complicated. In one sense, my theory is quite compatible with the restricted opportunity theory: it could be true both that, having little money, poor people get little relief from the marginal dollar and therefore often do not want to work, *and* that if all poor nonworkers wanted to work, there would be a significant shortage of jobs. Likewise for the opportunities to finish school, save, and so on. Both the will and the opportunity are necessary, but both could be missing. Yet in another sense, my theory tends to make the restricted opportunity theory less attractive. Chapter 3 cited survey evidence that poor people's opportunities to work and save in the United States are not restricted. Poor people themselves do not blame a lack of jobs for nonwork. Yet many observers discount this evidence, especially for minorities, postulating, for instance, that victims of discrimination have been to some degree deceived by a national myth of equal opportunity. But why do observers want to protect the restricted opportunity hypothesis in the first place? I believe that the restricted opportunity thesis (together with its protective postulates) draws much of its appeal from the following reasoning. Assuming, as we have good reasons to do, that poor nonworkers are rational, and that their tastes are typical, and that their choices are not distorted by public policy, then they *must* be suffering from restricted opportunity, because, seeing that their marginal utility for a dollar must be enormous, what else could possibly explain their nonwork? They have so much to gain that there must be an external obstacle. By rebutting the assumption that their marginal utility for a dollar must be enormous, my theory makes that conclusion avoidable, and this allows us to embrace the natural implication of the survey evidence, which is that opportunity restrictions are not a very important factor in nonwork. The same analysis holds mutatis mutandis for the restricted opportunity explanations of the remaining poverty-linked behaviors.

Similarly, my proposal is strictly consistent with the hypothesis that poor people engage in the poverty-linked behaviors on account of atypical preferences. It could be true both that becoming poor would make anyone more like Huck Finn and that the people who are in fact poor are more like Huck Finn than other people, at every income level. Analogously, someone with many uncured stings may refrain from working for a dab of salve both because his uncured stings reduce the value of a single dab and because he has a high pain tolerance. But at the same time my hypothesis reduces the appeal of the atypical preferences theory. Recall the empirical evidence against the atypical preferences theory that was cited in chapter 3. If the theory retains any appeal in the face of these data, that appeal may well stem from the reasoning that if poor people are rational, have full opportunities, and are not affected by bad public policy, then given how much more everyone stands to gain from the marginal dollar when poor than when rich, their nonwork must stem from a systematic difference — an atypically low interest in the things money can buy or an atypical interest in leisure at every income level. By rebutting the assumption that poverty increases the utility that an individual stands to gain from the marginal dollar, my theory makes this conclusion avoidable. So the natural conclusion from the survey evidence can be embraced after all: the tastes and tolerances of people who are poor do not in fact differ systematically from those of people who are not poor, but rather the utility gained from a dollar at each income level tends to be similar.[10]

As for where my proposal leaves the effort to trace poverty-linked conduct to bad public policy, I will defer this issue to chapter 7, where I consider the policy implications of the hypothesis that marginal utility rises amid true scarcity.

APPENDIX
Further Exploration Through Graphical Analysis

We can explore the implications of my hypothesis about marginal utility more fully with the help of some simple graphs. One such implication is that where the good being allocated is a reliever/pleaser and where the amount to be allocated could not do more than relieve misery even if devoted entirely to one of the rival uses, the efficient allocation is allocating it entirely to one of the rival uses. Contrary to marginalism, equimarginal allocation in such a case will actually be the utility-*minimizing* allocation. Recall, for instance, the case of the worker and her walk to work. Suppose she lives eight miles from her workplace and has bus fare that is sufficient to pay for six of those miles, and that this bus fare must last her for two days. The textbook strategy (predicated on diminishing marginal utility) is to buy a three-mile ride each day, but she can wring more relief from her bus fare by favoring one day or the other, since the distance she rides on the favored day beyond three miles adds more relief than the distance she loses on the disfavored day subtracts. To take just one possibility, she might divide her budget so that she walks seven miles one day and three the next, instead of walking five of the eight miles each day. This will probably help because the misery that a sixth and seventh blister/dish/reprimand add to the misery of five is likely to be small, but the relief of eliminating two out of five is likely to be noticeable.

These points can be clarified and confirmed by figure 5.1. Here the horizontal axis represents the worker's transportation budget for the two days, sixty cents. Possible allocations for Day One are shown on the horizontal scale, reading from left to right, while the amount that would be left over for Day Two is shown on the same scale, reading from right to left. The vertical axis represents marginal benefit, in this case relief. The marginal utility function AD shows the marginal utility for the passenger as a function of the amount that is spent for a ride on Day One, and it rises from the lower left to the upper right, in keeping with my hypothesis that the marginal utility of relief increases with use or consumption of the relieving good. The function EB represents the worker's marginal utility as a function of the amount for Day Two, and it likewise rises.

Plainly, the total utility of each possible allocation is represented by the sum of the areas under the two functions at that split point. For instance, if the split is determined by the rule of equimarginal allocation, then the budget is split at F. In that case the total relief derived from the budget is the sum of the relief that the passenger gets on Day One, namely, ACF, plus the relief the passenger gets on Day Two,

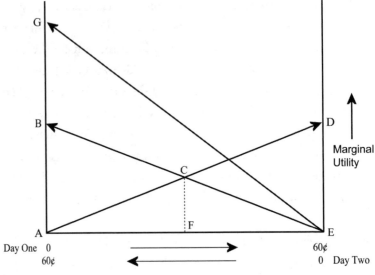

Figure 5.1.

namely, ECF. Note that this total, represented by the triangle ACE, is the smallest total utility that can be derived from the budget, since moving the split point away from F in either direction adds more area to ACE than it subtracts. Moreover, the net gain over equimarginal allocation grows as the split point diverges from F. Thus moving the split point from F all the way to E increases the utility received on Day One by FCDE, while it decreases the utility derived on Day Two by only FCE, for a net gain in utility of CDE. In fact, this move is one way to maximize the relief provided by the whole budget, as there is no larger area under the two functions than ADE. However, there is another area equally large, ABE, which indicates that all-for-one in either direction will maximize utility. A handy way to verify that both all-for-one splits maximize utility is to notice that the triangles ABC and CDE, which represent the advantages of the two extreme splits over the minimizing, equimarginal split, are equal in area. Note that no cardinal numbers for utilities need to be assumed to reach this result, as long as the functions are identical and rising.

Sticking with figure 5.1, consider next the marginal utility function EG. This represents the marginal utility function for a bus ride on Day Two if the price per mile is lower than on Day One. Each penny now buys her more miles on the bus, so EG slopes more steeply upward than AD, the function for Day One. Here again the utility-maximizing allocation is all-for-one, but it is no longer a matter of indifference which day is favored. Rather, the whole budget should be allocated to Day Two, since AGE is the largest area that can be contained under the two functions at any split point.

The same graphical approach — when combined with the new hypothesis about marginal utility — can also illuminate poor people's allocation of time and effort between work for pay and unpaid activity. While cases vary, we can illustrate with a case in which the marginal utility of paid work is increasing, while the marginal utility of unpaid activity is diminishing. This is not unrealistic. For instance, we can easily imagine a poor individual who has to allocate a forty-hour workweek between tending his own garden and tending his neighbor's garden for pay. We may suppose that his evenings and weekends, outside of the forty-hour week, afford him enough time to weed and clean up his own garden, which has increasing marginal benefit, like the washing of dishes discussed earlier. But his efforts in his own garden during the day from Monday until Friday go beyond relieving eyesores to nurturing beautiful plants, and this gives him positive experience that diminishes at the margin. (The twentieth blooming rose brings him less pleasure than the first, and so on.) On the other hand, equally arduous efforts in his neighbor's garden bring income. Since he is poor and will be poor even if he works for his

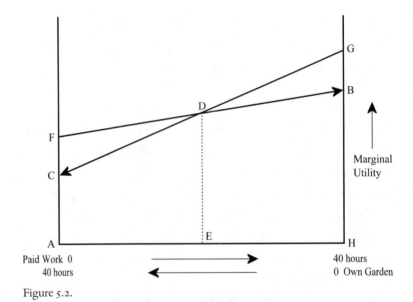

Figure 5.2.

neighbor all forty hours, his marginal utility from this activity is increasing. How should the forty hours be allocated?

Any of three answers is a possibility, depending on the heights and slopes of the utility functions for the paid and unpaid activities: that the hours should be allocated equimarginally, or that they should all be spent in his own garden, or that they should all be spent working for the neighbor. Does the theory's consistency with so many answers mean it is short on explanatory or predictive power? On the contrary, as we shall see in a moment.

Figures 5.2 and 5.3 clarify and confirm that all three answers are possible. In figure 5.2, FB represents the poor individual's marginal utility from time spent in paid gardening, which is increasing. GC represents the marginal utility of time spent working in his own garden, which is diminishing. Here the maximizing solution is equi-

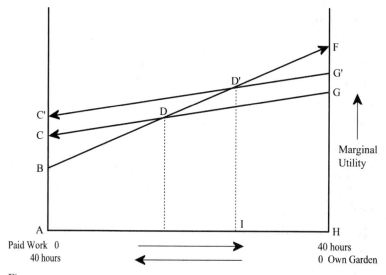

Figure 5.3.

marginal allocation of time, which is to say, working part-time in each garden, since the greatest possible area under the two functions is AFDE plus GDEH.

As in figure 5.2, so in figure 5.3 the marginal utility of time spent in paid gardening is BF, which is rising, and the marginal utility of time spent by the poor individual in his own garden is GC, which is diminishing. However, in this case equimarginal allocation *minimizes* the utility derived from forty hours. An all-for-one solution will maximize the utility. In this case, the better all-for-one solution is devoting all forty hours to paid work in the neighbor's garden, which is reflected in the fact that triangle BCD is smaller than triangle FDG. Putting it another way, the area ACGH is smaller than the area ABFH.

But now suppose that the poor allocator experiences a slight increase in the enjoyment he derives from time spent working in his own garden. Maybe he reads something that gives him a new appreciation of this activity, such as Voltaire's recommendation at the end of *Candide* to cultivate one's own garden. Specifically, suppose that the allocator's utility function for hours of working in his own garden shifts upward from GC to G'C'. Notice that this slight shift in his taste completely flips the recommended time allocation. Now the utility-maximizing allocation is devoting all forty hours to working in his own garden, rather than devoting all forty hours to working for his neighbor. To see this quickly, start by noting that the utility-minimizing allocation will be the equimarginal allocation, since ABD'I + D'IHG' is the smallest area that can be contained under the two functions. Note next that moving the split point in either direction away from I adds more area than it subtracts, and that the addition grows as the split point moves, meaning that the maximizing solution will be all-for-one. The remaining question, then, is whether the triangle BC'D' adds more to the minimizing allocation than the triangle D'FG'. (In other words, is AC'G'H bigger than ABFH?) Since BC'D' does add more, the maximizing allocation is to devote all forty hours to working in his own garden.

The significance of the fact that a slight preference shift completely flips the utility-maximizing time allocation is this: if poor people have increasing marginal utility for income, we do not have to assume much preference variation at all to make sense of the observed fact that significant numbers of poor people work for pay full-time and significant numbers do not work for pay at all. We have minimal need for what I called in chapter 3 the hypothesis of atypical preferences. By contrast, saddled with the assumption that marginal utility for income diminishes, conventional wisdom can rationalize voluntary unemployment on the part of poor people by invoking their preferences only if it hypothesizes that their preferences are *extremely* atypical. And this, I have argued, is unlikely.

The same kind of analysis can also rationalize another (supposedly) poverty-linked behavior that has helped popularize dysfunctionalism. This is the alleged preference of poor African Americans for luxurious cars plus very inadequate housing over the combination of cheaper cars and less inadequate housing. It is embodied in the stereotype of the shack with the Cadillac parked beside it, which dates to the early part of the twentieth century.[11] For the moment let us suspend judgment and just explore the implications of the stereotype. According to marginalism, it will be the first dollars spent on either transportation or housing that have the highest marginal utility. So a balanced allocation between the two uses would seem to be more efficient than splurging on the one and skimping on the other. Hence the Cadillac/shack stereotype launches a version of the familiar poverty debate: is the spending on automotive luxury a waste, traceable to pretension, maybe, or tricky automobile marketing? or is it the result of lack of opportunity to buy decent housing? or do poor African Americans have an unusual appreciation for cars?

But now notice what happens if we substitute the assumption that as long as housing is insufficient, the marginal utility of dollars for housing rises rather than falls. (Remember the story of the too-small house.) Then we can grant that housing is a very important good, one capable of bringing great relief and great positive satisfaction, and yet insist that the utility of housing dollars is *low* for poor people — not, again, because they are eccentric but simply because they cannot spend much on housing. If the utility of their housing dollars is indeed low, then even if the marginal utility of dollars they spend for automotive luxury is diminishing, still the total utility of buying a

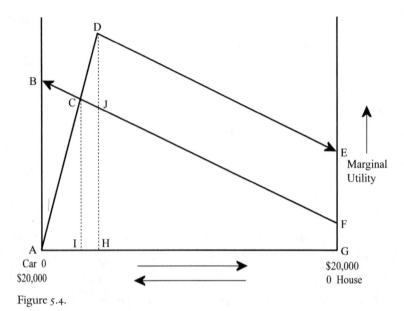

Figure 5.4.

luxury car and leaving the shack unimproved may be higher than the total utility of buying a merely sufficient car and fixing the shack.

Figure 5.4 illustrates a case of this. Here ADE, rising from the left and then falling to E, represents the marginal utility of dollars for a car, with D being the point where automotive spending verges into luxury. FB, rising from right to left, is marginal utility for dollars spent on housing. With these givens, consider first the utility of dividing a twenty-thousand-dollar budget for house and car at H, so that no more than "just enough" goes for the car and the rest goes for housing. This utility is equal to the area ADH + JHGF. Since ABC is greater than CJD, more would be gained than lost by moving the split point all the way to A, where housing receives the whole budget. But still more can be gained by moving the split point from H all the way to G, so that the car receives the whole budget. For now DJFE is added to the utility of splitting at H, and DJFE is a larger addition to the utility of splitting at H than (ABC - CJD). In short, on these assumptions, buying a luxury car while leaving the shack unimproved does not have to be seen as irrational, and it does not have to be rationalized by bringing in restricted opportunity or atypical tastes, because buying a luxury car while leaving the shack unimproved turns out to be rational in the first place.

6

Responses to Challenges
and Questions

I will now respond to a number of challenges and questions. For brevity's sake I shall state my replies with few of the qualifications normally found in academic debate.

If your theory is correct, why isn't it conventional wisdom already? After all, the main evidence you cite is introspected experience, and that is available to everybody. How could the fact that relievers have increasing marginal benefit have escaped the notice of the marginalists — and their followers?

I think the marginalists got the wrong answer not because they introspected inaccurately (assuming that even makes sense), but because they failed to ask the oracle of introspection the right question. (This is a common problem with oracles.) They asked how feelings of positive satisfaction change as someone consumes increasing amounts of pleasers and then wrongly assumed that the answer — that feelings of positive satisfaction grow at a diminishing rate — applies equally to the question of how feelings of relief change as someone consumes increasing amounts of relievers. The marginalists should have asked the reliever question separately, but they didn't, and the reason they didn't is that they did not see that it was a distinct question.

Why not? Because they reasoned about marginal utility under the influence of the prevailing philosophy of their own day, the utilitarianism of Jeremy Bentham and John Stuart Mill (1806–73). Disastrously, Bentham often and Mill consistently equated happiness with the relief of unhappiness. A good name for this mistake is the Epicurean Fallacy because it was an explicit doctrine of the Athenian philosopher Epicurus (341–270 B.C.), and Epicurus was a major influence on Mill by way of his father, James Mill (1773–1836), who greatly admired Epicurus. Epicurus regarded happiness as the reciprocal of misery, in the sense that fullness is the reciprocal of emptiness, and tallness is the reciprocal of shortness: increases in the one can just as well be seen as decreases in the other.[1] Just as more full means less empty, and taller means less short, so happier was thought to mean less unhappy — and vice versa. Perfect happiness, if it exists, would be the complete lack of unhappiness, and perfect unhappiness would be the complete lack of happiness.[2] This plainly entails that to relieve unhappiness and to cause happiness are simply alternative names for the same process. But this means in turn that *goods* that serve as relievers of unhappiness and goods that serve as bringers of happiness must be the same things by different names. Relievers are pleasers, and pleasers are relievers.

Mill can be found embracing the Epicurean Fallacy when he says that martyrs are people who "voluntarily do without happiness" and who make an "absolute sacrifice of happiness."[3] Of course, martyrs endure a lot worse than just the lack of happiness, unless we equate lack of happiness with extreme misery, as Mill must be doing. One

place where Bentham too falls into the Epicurean Fallacy is his definition of "utility" as "that property in any object whereby it tends to
produce . . . pleasure . . . or happiness . . . or *(what comes to the same
thing)* to prevent the happening of mischief, pain, evil, or unhappiness."[4] This passage is particularly significant for our purposes because the influential marginalist W. Stanley Jevons cites it eighty years
later as the best available definition of the concept of utility, the maximization of which he considers the aim of economics.[5] In short,
Bentham's error in this passage may well have played a role in Jevons's
own acceptance of the Epicurean Fallacy. But usually Bentham is not
taken in by this fallacy. A more typical statement would be his assertion that one can determine the goodness or badness of an act by
determining the balance of pleasure over pain or of pain over pleasure
that the act causes.[6] Such a calculation of the net of pleasure and pain
clearly presupposes that there exists a hedonic zero point separating a
positive range from a negative range, which is a supposition entirely
incompatible with the Epicurean Fallacy.

The mischief of the Epicurean Fallacy was that information about
the marginal rate at which pleasers please was seen as ipso facto information about the marginal rate at which relievers relieve. After all, if
they were the same thing by different names, then what was true of
one had to be true of the other. If the marginal benefit of pleasing
dollars for Bill Gates was diminishing, then the marginal benefit of
relieving dollars for the family in the homeless shelter had to be diminishing too. Generally, if the law of diminishing marginal utility
described the impact of dessert-like goods, it had to describe the
impact of salve-like goods as well. No need for a separate introspection of the marginal impact of salve-like goods was recognized. This is
probably how the law of diminishing marginal utility came to be
accepted as a general truth.

Theoretically, of course, the Epicurus-influenced marginalists might have generalized in the other direction. They might have introspected the marginal benefit of relievers, determined it was increasing, and simply assumed it would be increasing for pleasers too because they saw pleasers as relievers by another name. But the marginalists, like theorists in every age, were drawn from the financially comfortable classes. They were used to consumption of basic goods at pleasing levels. Not surprisingly, then, they started with the introspectible datum that pleasers have diminishing marginal benefit and saw no need to look further. An example of this from a precursor of the marginalists is the passage I quoted in chapter 4, in which Bentham, who was himself well-off, supports the notion that marginal utility diminishes generally by considering "the matter of wealth," and what happens when one multiplies "a man's property" by a thousand.[7] Marginalist economics was an economics of more-than-enough that mistook itself for a general theory, applicable to both surplus and deficit. It was an economics of happiness that saw itself as an economics of both happiness and misery.[8]

Had happiness and misery really been related in the way that the Epicurus-influenced economists believed, of course, their generalization of the law of diminishing marginal utility from pleasers to relievers would have been no different than extending the answer to the question, "How fast does the pipe fill the tub?" to the question, "How fast does the pipe make the tub less empty?" But — I will argue in a moment — the Epicurean Fallacy is a *fallacy,* and therein lies the problem with generalizing from the marginal utility of pleasers. Happiness and unhappiness are not reciprocals. More of one does not mean less of the other. Rather, they are polars, like optimism and pessimism and like saintliness and devilishness. They range out in opposite directions from a neutral condition. Just as less pessimistic does not mean more optimistic, less unhappy does not mean more happy.[9] There is an equator to be crossed in both cases before improvements take you into a positive zone. So we cannot equate goods that *cause* reductions in unhappiness with goods that *cause* increases in happiness. Relievers are not pleasers by another name, but a distinct class of goods or at least a distinct level of the same goods. Therefore we cannot assume that the marginal rate at which pleasers accomplish their work is the marginal rate at which relievers accomplish theirs. Assuming this would be like assuming that the rate at which pep talks make optimists more optimistic is automatically that at which they make pessimists less pessimistic; or that the rate at which sermons make saintly people more saintly is automatically the rate at which they make diabolical people less diabolical.

As for how the mistake made its way from the early utilitarians to the marginalists, the carrier seems to have been the concept of utility itself. "Utility" originally meant "happiness"—but happiness conceived as Bentham sometimes and Mill consistently conceived it, that is, as the reciprocal of misery, not its polar opposite. To adopt that infected term, as marginalists like Jevons and, later, Alfred Marshall did, was virtually to accept the conception of happiness and unhappiness as reciprocals. While later economists stripped some of the psychological connotations from the term, the mischievous consequence of the Epicurean Fallacy has persisted—the assumption that what we know about pleasers' marginal benefit must be just as true for relievers.

What, then, is the case against Epicurus? How do we know that the Epicurean Fallacy is a fallacy? The Irish philosopher Edmund Burke (1729–97) argued as follows: "There is nothing which I can distinguish in my mind with more clearness than the three states of indifference, of pleasure, and of pain. Every one of these I can perceive without any sort of idea of its relation to any thing else. Caius is afflicted with a fit of the cholic; this man is actually in pain; stretch Caius upon the rack, he will feel a much greater pain; but does this pain of the rack arise from the removal of any pleasure?"[10] By the same token, suppose a runner whose life's ambition is to win a medal at the Olympics is standing on the dais having the silver medal hung around her neck. She is beaming. Suddenly the judges announce that they have made a mistake, and she has in fact won the gold medal. Would we say that the woman is made less unhappy by the news?

As another argument, imagine a blissfully happy man with no romantic dimension to his life whatsoever. He is not romantically happy or unhappy, in other words, but simply oblivious to romance. Suddenly the man gets trapped in an extremely unhappy romance. If the Epicurean view were correct, and unhappiness were the same as a low level of happiness, then it should be acceptable to describe the unhappy romance as bringing a little romantic happiness into his life. Should he then celebrate, with beer if not champagne? But on our givens, the romance makes him less happy on balance, and we would expect the man to exit the relationship rather than celebrating.

Finally, phenomenological ammunition against Epicurus, so to speak, was supplied by a later utilitarian, Henry Sidgwick (1838–1900), in his description of the "hedonic zero" or neutral state — a state that would not exist altogether, of course, if the reciprocals view were correct. In the following passage, Sidgwick makes the subtle point that the hedonic zero is not our default condition. This may help explain why its very existence was overlooked by the supporters of the Epicurean view. Simply, it is not a condition in which we find ourselves normally: "Experience seems to show that a state very nearly approximating to . . . [hedonic zero] is even common: and we certainly experience continued transitions from pleasure to pain and vice versa, and thus . . . we must exist at least momentarily in this neutral state. . . . But it would, I think, be equally erroneous . . . to regard . . . [hedonic zero] as the normal condition of our consciousness, out of which we occasionally sink into pain, and occasionally rise into pleasure. Nature has not been so niggardly to man as this . . . the mere performance of the ordinary habitual functions of life is, according to my experience, a frequent source of moderate pleasures."[11]

> *Your argument is that as more and more problems are relieved, attention will be concentrated on those problems that remain, making successive relievers ever more effective. Such an "attention effect" may indeed be the key factor in determining the marginal utility of goods that relieve uniform or homogeneous evils or burdens, like the pounds of grain in the sack that has to be carried up the hill. But when the evils or burdens to be relieved vary in their severity, won't a rational poor person deploy his resources on the most serious problems first, working down the list to the least serious? Hence it would seem that the marginal benefit of reliever goods will diminish, not increase.*

To clarify before I reply, suppose that hunger is the most important of someone's problems and lack of education is second on the list, and suppose that both problems cost x dollars (or hours) to alleviate. Then if the person is sensible, he will attack hunger first and education second. Therefore he will get more relief from the first x dollars than from the second x dollars. And the same reasoning will hold for each problem considered individually. Taking hunger, for instance, the rational poor person will use her first dollar on the most trying of her food shortages, and she will use her second dollar to buy the food she hungers for next most intensely, and so on, with the result that each dollar used for food will have less impact than the previous dollar. In short, because rational people "put out the hottest fire first," the marginal utility of relievers is diminishing and not increasing, as I have claimed.

In reply, I would say that the objection is weak on its face if it means that the attention effect is irrelevant to the question of the marginal utility of relievers. A more plausible version is that with many or most relievers there is a more important, countervailing factor: that the tendency of rational people to prioritize the most severe problems will tend to mean that as a series of problems is relieved, the marginal relief becomes smaller and smaller. The real point of disagreement must be, which factor is generally more important in determining the marginal utility of relievers? Is it "the hottest fire first" factor (the prioritization effect)? or is it the "first subtracted pound is least noticeable" factor (the attention effect)?

One reason to think that *amid scarcity* the attention effect is normally stronger than the prioritization effect is that whereas people tend to be connoisseurs when it comes to the sources of their positive pleasures, they tend to be undiscriminating about the things that relieve their miseries. Pleasers are specific, relievers are generic. For instance, the person who is drinking for pleasure may feel a strong and definite preference for red wine over white, or the other way around, but the person who is drinking to relieve thirst wants "something to drink," and he may even say, "Whatever you've got." The person at the buffet who is eating for pleasure may feel and act on a definite preference for the shrimp over the roast beef, or the other way around, but the famished person will tend to load up at the first serving station he comes to. The person who sees friends every evening will prefer Smith to Jones on a particular evening, but the lonely person is "starved for *company*" and will tend to chat with the first person who comes along. The traveler who intends to enjoy a quiet evening in his hotel room may test both beds to see which he prefers, but the traveler who stumbles in exhausted will fall on the bed nearest the door.

While it may be true that beggars can't be choosers, the point in these examples is that in moments of neediness, we tend not to be choosy even when we can afford to be. Our miseries are broad targets, easily hit by any of a wide range of relievers. This fact helps to explain the tendency of almost all governments (Imperial Rome being a possible exception) to promote the welfare of their citizens by relieving dissatisfactions rather than enhancing satisfactions: it is more efficient to relieve than to please, in part because the target is easier to hit.

Well, so what? The key point here is that even when goods *can* be discriminated and prioritized, *in fact* we tend to notice and care about the differences to the extent they are serving as pleasers and to overlook and downplay the differences to the extent that they are serving as relievers. Hence we do not tend to consume goods, qua relievers, in rank order of felt benefit. We tend to experience them as relatively uniform or homogeneous, like the lightenings of the sack of grain, and so we consume them in any convenient order or randomly. Of course, prioritization may occur with relievers too. We may salve the sting on the lip before the sting on the back. But the point is that discrimination and prioritization are less significant with relievers than with pleasers. But if there is little prioritization among relievers in the first place, we should expect the attention effect to be weightier than the prioritization effect in determining whether the marginal utility of relievers is rising or falling. In short, it should lead us to expect the marginal utility of relievers to be rising.

Such psychological observations, informal as they are, give reason to think that the marginal utility of relieving goods is rising, not falling. They weigh on the same side as the advantages of my hypothesis mentioned in earlier chapters — the survey evidence against restricted opportunity, the parsimoniousness of ascribing efficiency to human conduct in general, the parsimoniousness of assuming that human beings have similar tastes and preferences, and so forth. With regard to income itself, as distinct from particular goods, there is also more direct survey evidence for increasing marginal utility amid scarcity, which is less well known in the United States than it should be. Beginning in the 1970s, the so-called Leyden school of economists administered a series of surveys in Europe. In these surveys individuals were asked to identify after-tax monthly incomes that they would describe negatively or positively. In recent versions the scale has been *very bad, bad, insufficient, sufficient, good,* and *very good.* It has emerged that the intervals between the incomes described by each of these six labels first grow larger and then shrink, as respondents move from very bad to very good. Research showed further that respondents tend to treat the labels as marking equal subjective or hedonic differences. A fair inference from these facts is that respondents' marginal utilities for income are rising at low levels of income and falling at high levels. In the mildly worded summary of one article by members of this school, "The [utility] function is not concave for all income levels, but convex for low incomes. This runs counter to mainstream economic assumptions."[12]

But how did the increasing marginal utility of relievers escape the notice of the marginalists? Part of the answer may be implicit in the answer to the previous question. As we have already seen, thinkers in the early utilitarian tradition, including economists, generally seem to have underappreciated the distinction between pleasers and relievers and between reliever/pleasers at the two levels. What holds for goods serving as pleasers was automatically assumed to hold for goods serving as relievers. I do not think it is too much to conjecture that this led marginalists to overgeneralize from the usual practice in their own economic stratum—that of sharply discriminating and prioritizing among goods serving as pleasers—and so to overestimate the degree to which poor people do the same thing with goods serving as relievers. From this overestimate it is a short step, of course, to the conclusion that the prioritization effect dominates the attention effect in determining the marginal utility of relievers—and to the further conclusion that relievers' marginal utility must be diminishing.

> *Solving some of the problems that typically face poor people often helps to solve others. Relieving a poor child's hunger, for instance, may reduce her problems in school. Health care may increase earnings. Earnings may increase the chances of forming stable partnerships. Etc. Because the severity of a particular problem that faces an impoverished allocator will often be affected in this way by its place in the order of problems being addressed, the marginal benefit of resources deployed on successive problems will tend to diminish.*

But assuming that the earlier solutions reduce the severity of the later problems does not show that the marginal utility of resources will tend to diminish, unless one also assumes that the severity of the later problems will decrease without a proportional reduction in the resources that would have otherwise been needed to relieve those later problems. Perhaps it is true, for instance, that a school lunch program will increase a poor child's mental acuity and therefore improve his or her reading skills. But the same increase in acuity will also presumably make the resources that are used to teach the child to read—teaching time, textbooks—more effective, so that less of them is needed. And it may cut the funds needed for teaching and textbooks by an amount that is out of proportion to the direct reduction in the severity of the problem. In short, the objection gives no reason to think that bang for the teaching and textbook buck will be diminished on balance by addressing hunger first. Indeed, advocates for various types of aid to the poor — from school lunches to health care — almost always present evidence that the favored type of aid will catalyze the resources needed for other problems, raising and not lowering the efficiency of those resources.

If income is the key to allocation behavior, as you claim, then why do people with different incomes often behave similarly, and why do people with the same incomes often behave differently?

Here I would repeat a point made earlier: that whether something is functioning as a reliever for a given consumer is relative. It is only partly a question of objective economic circumstances, because it depends too upon how the consumer sees those circumstances. One person's "reliever level" income is another person's "pleaser level" income.

Thus, two people with different incomes who both count as very poor because their incomes fall comparably short of the levels considered sufficient in their respective societies should be expected to allocate similarly. For instance, we should not be surprised if an American with an income of twenty thousand dollars and a Pole with an income of five thousand dollars both allocate a big fraction of time to unpaid pursuits, drop out of school, fail to save, and take undue economic risks. For we may suppose that they are both benefit maximizers who see their different incomes as very, and similarly, insufficient and as bringing increasing marginal relief. Different numbers of stings when combined with different pain sensitivities can hurt about the same, making it rational to spend the same effort for a dab of salve and to budget one's salve the same way.

Contrast this with the supposition that distinct causes explain the similar behaviors of the poor in rich and poor nations. For instance, Lawrence Mead contends that nonwork in the developing world is a matter of limited job opportunities, while nonwork in the United States is a matter of dysfunction.[13] Granted, similar effects may stem from different causes. But parsimony inclines us to look for similar causes first. Moreover, even if the hypothesis of varying local causes for global behaviors were correct for nonwork, it surely wears thinner with repeated use. What about the global pervasiveness among the poor of low educational achievement, uneven consumption, and risk taking? Does each of these have different causes in different locations?

That painfulness and pleasurability are relative to the perceiver sheds light on another fact as well. In recent years the "behavioral" school of economics has stressed that not only the poor but members of the middle class in every society engage in seemingly irrational conduct, such as failing to save enough, even if at a lower rate than the poor.[14] Why? I think this is illuminated by the relativity of a good's being a reliever or a pleaser to the norms and expectations of the perceiver. I noted in chapter 1 that a well-off person—for instance, a millionaire in the United States—whose experience or temperament makes his income feel insufficient to him does not count as poor, given the dependence of "poverty" on what is *typically* regarded as insufficient. Nevertheless, the fact that dollars for such a person function as relievers may rationalize what appear to be economically irrational behaviors, such as failure to save.

What about the much-discussed fact that equally poor people in a given society may allocate very differently? For instance, some poor people in the United States work full-time, avidly pursue education, and save significant portions of their income, while others go to opposite extremes. To some extent this coincides with immigrant status and with ethnic and racial differences. Observers explain these facts in different ways. From the perspective of a Benjamin Franklin, poor people who work hard, study hard, save, remain sober, and conduct themselves honestly are responsible and disciplined individuals who maximize the benefit of their time and money, while poor people who do not conduct themselves this way are simply undisciplined and wasteful. Modern liberals, by contrast, tend to downplay differences in personal qualities and instead stress differences in opportunity owing to prejudice against certain groups of poor people or simple luck. A more anthropological view responds that the difference lies in neither discipline nor opportunity but in the values of the various subcultures. Supposedly, members of some groups are acculturated to a strong work ethic, the importance of self-support, and the value of education, while members of other groups are not acculturated to these values. Within this anthropological view we see a further distinction. On the one hand there is a moralistic version, which disapproves of the presumed rejection of the work ethic and the values of education and saving, etc.; and on the other hand there is a relativistic version, which notes the supposed difference in values without judging one set of values to be better than another.

My hypothesis in this book suggests yet a fourth possibility. No one doubts that different cultural groups within the United States have different histories, and that these different histories create different economic norms and expectations. For instance, having come from much poorer countries, Asian immigrants to the United States often have relatively low norms and expectations. By contrast, African Americans, who are closely acquainted with the lifestyles of middle-class whites, and who have long been exposed to "the American dream" and all it implies, often have relatively high norms, if not exactly expectations. As a result, Asian immigrants with low incomes are probably less unhappy with their economic situation than African Americans in similar straits.[15] When taken together with my hypothesis that the marginal benefit of income is increasing for poor people, this difference in norms and expectations predicts that the felt relief from the marginal dollar will be greater for poor Asian immigrants than the felt relief from the marginal dollar for similarly poor African Americans. So we should expect poor Asian immigrants to be more willing to do low-wage jobs than equally poor African Americans. This predicted situation is precisely what we see in fact.

To put it in terms of stings and salve, a poor Asian immigrant may regard an annual income of twenty thousand dollars as verging on sufficient—as leaving just a few stings unsalved—while a poor African American may regard that same income as very insufficient—as leaving so many stings uncured that it is not worth much effort to get another dab or two of salve. The same number of stings plus different degrees of sensitivity yield different levels of pain, making different allocations of salve equally rational.

Like the capacities, opportunities, and cultural values theories, this theory too can account for the correlation of allocation behavior with subculture, ethnicity, and race. But rather than saying that cultural differences operate independently of income, my theory proposes that cultural differences impact behavior by impacting the way income is perceived. Subculture, or, more exactly, the norms and expectations that are linked with subculture, should be seen as a prism or lens, not as an independent variable. Behavioral differences are to be explained as equally rational, benefit-maximizing responses to the same economic facts, seen and felt differently.

This can be turned into an argument in favor of my hypothesis about the marginal utility of income amid poverty. Grant that an individual's norms and expectations strongly affect how happy or unhappy he or she will be with a given level of income. Then the law of diminishing marginal utility should make us expect low-income Asian immigrants to put a *lower* priority on paid employment than low-income African Americans. After all, they are less unhappy. But in fact they put a *higher* priority on paid employment than low-income African Americans. That my hypothesis predicts what is actually the case, while the law of diminishing marginal utility predicts the opposite, supports the hypothesis.

> *Isn't there a psychological tendency to normalize the status quo, the so-called process of adaptation? But that means that extra resources, over and above the individual's usual level of consumption, will always be pleasers — unless and until the higher level of consumption itself becomes habitual. So if the marginal utility of pleasers is diminishing, as you have certainly admitted, then even poor people will experience improvements as having diminishing marginal utility. The marginal utility of consumption amid poverty is not generally increasing, therefore.*

It is often said that human beings tend to normalize the status quo and see all gains relative to that point as pleasers and all losses relative to that point as sources of misery.[16] This is part of what's funny in the story of the rabbi who urges a miserable follower to take a goat into his house. After a week the follower comes back, and the rabbi tells him to let the goat out again. "There," says the rabbi, "aren't you happier now?"

Strong interest in this "where one starts" variable in recent years is due to the work of the psychologists Daniel Kahneman and Amos Tversky. Their experiments with small wagers showed that subjects preferred risk over actuarially equivalent certainty when it came to losses, but that subjects preferred certainty over risk when it came to gains.[17] This led them to conclude that the negative marginal impact of lost goods was diminishing, and the positive marginal impact of gained goods was also diminishing. Graphically, they postulated an S-shaped utility function with an inflection point that floated up or down with the starting point. If Kahneman's and Tversky's hypothesis accurately describes the psychology of people in general, then the hypothesis of this book, that small consumption gains tend to produce increasing marginal utility below the socially defined poverty line, is incorrect.

To start with a point of agreement, it follows from the relativity of poverty that I insisted on in chapter 1 that the inflection point of the utility function in my hypothesis — the point at which marginal utility ceases to rise and begins to diminish — is not pinned to any particular level of consumption. My inflection point floats too. That is because the consumption level that counts as just enough to meet basic needs varies from society to society and from age to age, as norms, expectations, and possibilities vary. In the United States, the growing economy itself has brought new goods within the reach of the average person. Indoor plumbing was a pleaser for many in 1920, but it is certainly a reliever today.

However, despite Kahneman's and Tversky's experiments, I doubt that the inflection point of the utility function floats with the individual's status quo. In particular, I do not believe that people are risk-averse over gains when the good in question is one that relieves real misery. If you had two stings and a dab of salve that could cure just one of the stings, thereby relieving only a small fraction of your pain, wouldn't you risk that dab in a fair double-or-nothing bet? I would. (If you think you would not, suppose the single dab relieved only a hundredth of your pain.) But to opt for the risk is to say that your utility function for salve is not diminishing over gains after all. The plausibility of the Kahneman and Tversky experiments seems to rest on the fact that the trivial sums and inexpensive trinkets employed were not relieving real misery. Their impact was determined entirely by their relation to the status quo, so gaining them was always a source of positive experience. It appears to me that in the real world of bigger sums, once social norms are factored in, the reliefs and pleasures of particular consumption levels are so significant that the starting point of the consumer shrinks greatly as a factor in allocation behavior.

Readers impressed with the adaptive capacities of human beings may think I have underestimated the starting point factor. But there is yet another argument against the floating inflection point hypothesis of Kahneman and Tversky. The economic concerns of allocators within each income band in the real world must be pretty evenly divided between upside and downside concerns. Hence the Kahneman and Tversky hypothesis predicts no pattern whatsoever in the allocation behaviors of people within a given income band. But this is contrary to fact. For instance, while the Kahneman and Tversky hypothesis does not predict disproportionate risk-taking among people in the lower income bands, it is empirically observed. To patch this problem, defenders of the Kahneman and Tversky hypothesis would have to say either that income-band-related behavioral differences stem from other causes; or that poor people are disproportionately inclined toward risk because they are mainly concerned with decisions affecting possible losses. Neither is compelling.

Some of your key examples involve so-called lumpy goods. Since the components of lumpy goods lack utility altogether, they are not goods whose utility grows by bigger and bigger amounts as they accumulate.

Let me state the objection more fully.[18] It says, first, that some of the goods from which I have generalized in my effort to show that relievers typically have increasing marginal utility belong to the category that economists call lumpy goods. A good is said to be lumpy when the consumer must consume a critical mass or threshold amount of its components in order to get the normal benefit, classical examples being pairs of shoes or sets of four automobile tires. The cases I have given that are in dispute include the repairs of scratches on a car, the washings of dishes in the sink, and the elimination of discrimination.

The objection goes on to say that the disputed cases fit the definition of a lumpy good. Supposedly, for instance, the good that the consumer really values in the car scratch case is *an unblemished finish*. Likewise the consumer really wants *an immaculate sink* and *a nondiscriminatory society*. These ideal or perfect conditions, which are what is really valued, are not themselves matters of degree. The sink is immaculate or it is not, and so on. Therefore the "subliminal" components of these ideal conditions—the individual scratch repairs, dish washings, and reforms—do not have the relevant kind of value. In this respect they are like each of the first three tires in the set of four or the first shoe of the pair. Only the component that brings the consumer up to the critical mass or threshold (the fourth tire, the second shoe, the dish washing that achieves immaculateness) has the relevant kind of utility. What I have done in the disputed cases, supposedly, is simplistically to compare the benefit of the first component, namely, none, with the benefit of the good-completing component, which is great, and then interpolate for all the components in between, to reach the unjustified conclusion that the components display steadily increasing marginal utility. Then I have generalized from these false cases to relievers in general.

Before I answer, an important clarification of the objection would be to underline that the benefit that the subliminal components of a lumpy good lack is the particular benefit that is *normally* sought from the complete good. The lumpy good idea does not say that the components lack all value, in other words, but only the usual value of the whole. For instance, you might make a nice planter out of your second tire, or sell it, or take heart from the fact that you are one tire closer to having a set. But the key point is that as you accumulate tires up to four, you do not get increments of the benefit of being able to drive your car.

The objection is wrong to say that what the consumer normally wants in the cited cases is perfection and nothing less. For instance, normally what we want from our cleaning efforts is cleanliness. Cleanliness, unlike immaculateness, comes in degrees. Immaculateness is the most valued degree of cleanliness, of course, and a single unwashed dish will reduce our satisfaction by a lot, precisely because as a single dish it will be much noticed. But even short of immaculateness, more cleanliness is preferred to less. And this is not just because each washed dish raises the chances of getting to the lumpy good of immaculateness, as is clear from the fact that even if we know, somehow, that we will not get to a perfectly clean sink, we are not indifferent to seeing *some* of the dishes get washed. We will take what we can get. So we will normally prefer nine dirty dishes to ten *for the same reason* that we prefer none to one: we like cleanliness. The only difference here is that the step between ten and nine will give us less perceived improvement than the step from one to none, due to the attention effect. This distinguishes the dishes case from the tires case: if we prefer two tires to one, it will be *for a different reason* than the reason we prefer a fourth tire to a third, such as that we want to make a planter out of it, sell it, or get encouragement from it.

A similar distinction can be drawn between the good of living in a perfectly nondiscriminatory society and the paradigm lumpy goods. It would be unusual and perhaps even morally frivolous to value perfection and nothing less. What is normally valued is nondiscrimination. Nondiscrimination in all areas of life is the most preferred situation, naturally, but less discrimination is better than more. We prefer a society with a little discrimination to a society with more discrimination for the same reason we prefer a society with none to a society with a little: we do not like discrimination. This is not parallel to the case with the tires or the shoes, where any preference for more of the component over less, below the threshold, depends on our seeking a different benefit than the benefit normally sought from the completed good.

So in each of my cases, unlike the components of lumpy goods, what we see are individual items (scratch repairs, dish washings, reforms) which bestow increasing utility as they accumulate, all the way up to a limiting case. Seeing that the objection fails to disprove steadily increasing utility in these cases, it also does not disprove that there is utility that grows at an increasing rate. True, the lumpy-good objection could be revised to say that while consumers do indeed place value on less-than-optimal levels of cleanliness, unblemishedness, and social nondiscrimination, that is only because the real threshold consumers seek is "a decent amount" and not perfection. But my answer is the same: if these were really threshold goods, then consumers would be indifferent between much less than decent levels and slightly less than decent levels. But consumers prefer more to less.

Granting the possible exception of Herodotus's Lydians, do not many great books from the ancient world implicitly support the law of diminishing marginal utility? For they endorse consumption smoothing over time. Surely these texts would not have survived in the referendum of history if they did not reflect the hard lessons of human experience.

Elaborating on the objection, one example is the story of Joseph in chapter 41 of the book of Genesis, who preserved Egypt during seven years of famine by setting corn aside during seven years of plenty. Further, there is Aesop's fable of the ant and the grasshopper, mentioned earlier. The ant lays corn aside during the summer and is enabled to eat in the winter, while the grasshopper, who eats all the corn he has during the luxurious summer, goes hungry in the winter. Yet a third example is book 4, chapter 1 of *Nicomachean Ethics,* in which Aristotle confidently observes that because people "soon exhaust all their substance" by prodigality, prodigal people will be "easily cured by poverty" and moved to the middle way between overspending and underspending. The common message seems to be that human beings should avoid having to underconsume by a certain amount in some situations by not overconsuming by that amount in other situations. Splurging is not worth the skimping that goes with it, because the pain from the shortfalls will be greater than the pleasures from the corresponding surpluses.

To respond, I grant that such a message follows from the law of diminishing marginal utility. For that supposed law directly entails that exceeding any average level of consumption by x at some times and falling short by x at others wastes potential utility. And this in turn entails, as one particular case, what these three texts seem to say: that for those who are in a position to consume just enough consistently, consuming more than enough at some times and a corresponding amount less than enough at other times wastes utility.

But that does not prove the point at issue, which is whether these durable texts implicitly support the law of diminishing marginal utility. For even if the law of diminishing marginal utility entails that it is wasteful to consume in a splurge/skimp fashion — that is, to vary consumption above and below sufficiency by equal amounts — the reverse implication does not hold. The doctrine that it is wasteful to splurge and skimp by equal amounts does not entail the law of diminishing marginal utility. On the contrary, the common doctrine of the

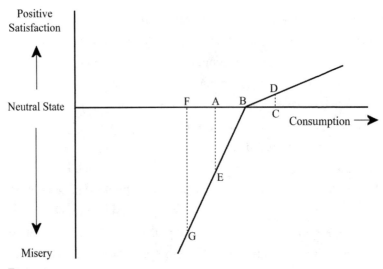

Figure 6.1.

three texts is consistent with any of a number of theories about the relation between consumption and well-being.

For instance, one such theory is that the marginal utility of surplus consumption is constant and that the marginal misery of deficient consumption is constant as well, but the pain of an x-sized deficit is simply greater than the pleasure of an x-sized surplus. An instance of this hypothesis is given in figure 6.1. Here consumption is shown on the horizontal axis and total utility is shown on the vertical axis, which is segmented into misery and positive satisfaction, with the intermediate condition of being neither unhappy nor happy at their interface. Just sufficient consumption occurs at B. BC represents a certain amount of luxurious consumption or splurging, and BA is an identical amount of skimping. Note that the positive satisfaction from luxurious consumption, which is CD, is less than AE, which is the misery from a correspondingly large insufficiency of consumption. Thus on the hypothesis shown in figure 6.1, it is imprudent to splurge if one has to skimp by just as much to make up for it.

But now consider the consumer who cannot avoid skimping just by not splurging — that is, the consumer whose total resources afford no opportunity to consume more than enough. On the hypothesis shown in figure 6.1, such a consumer neither loses nor gains by consuming unevenly: for instance, consuming barely enough one day and skimping a lot the next day produces no more or less misery over the long term than consuming at a midpoint each day. This is illustrated by the fact that the total misery from consuming all the way down at F on one day and at B the next day is the same as the misery from consuming at the midpoint, A, on each day — since FG is twice AE. In other words, the hypothesis in figure 6.1 does not imply that the practices of the Lydians or of present-day poor people who consume unevenly are more efficient for them than consumption smoothing would be. In that sense, it sheds no light on these practices.

Is there a way to make sense of these poverty-linked patterns, while *also* rationalizing the ancient proscription on skimp/splurge consumption? Yes, we might adopt either of the hypotheses shown in figure 6.2. Both are, of course, versions of the theory I have been arguing for throughout this book: that marginal utility rises below sufficiency and falls above it. On both of these hypotheses the dissatisfactions caused by a given amount of deprivation are bigger than the positive satisfactions caused by the same amount of luxury (just as in the first hypothesis). And what is more, on both hypotheses both the marginal misery caused by consumption shortfalls and the marginal positive satisfaction of above-sufficient consumption are diminishing. This latter point implies that consuming barely enough on one day and skimping greatly the next yields less misery in the long run than

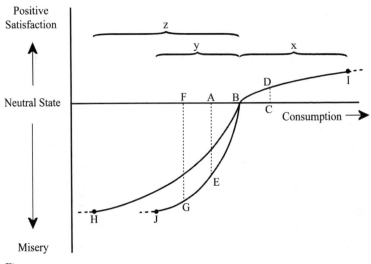

Figure 6.2.

skimping each day at the midpoint. Graphically, this is evident from the fact that while shortfall FB is twice shortfall AB, the misery caused by FB is less than twice the misery caused by AB. Namely, FG is less than twice AE.

The two functions in figure 6.2 are surely very significant, for they resolve the apparent tension between Herodotus on the one hand and Genesis, Aesop, and Aristotle on the other. It is true that Herodotus recommends uneven consumption while the latter three recommend consumption smoothing. But Herodotus is talking about consumption amid scarcity, while the latter three texts are talking about splurging and skimping around sufficiency. Again, both positions can in fact be rationalized by adopting hypotheses like those shown in figure 6.2. The biblical/Aesopian/Aristotelian conception of prudence turns out to be consistent with the Lydian conception of prudence after all and with the rationality of the behavior of poor people in many times and nations. This makes the hypotheses illustrated in figure 6.2 very attractive.

The next question is, are the two hypotheses in figure 6.2 equally attractive? On the contrary, common observation suggests that the version comprising JB should be preferred to the version comprising HB. For note that in the case of HBI, the income needed to take someone from the extremes of poverty-induced misery to complete relief, shown as z, exceeds the income required to take someone from the hedonically neutral point, B, to the extremes of wealth-caused positive satisfaction, shown as x. But this is utterly inconsistent with general opinion, which is that it takes very little to relieve the misery of poverty and an enormous amount to get from hedonic neutrality to the heights of wealth-based positive satisfaction. The common view is illustrated by the function JBI, in which the horizontal run from the asymptote of the lower limb to the inflection point, shown as y, is less than the horizontal run from the inflection point to the asymptote of the upper limb, shown as x.

Is the idea that resources have increasing marginal utility below sufficiency really new?

Readers with an interest in the history of ideas may wonder about the origins of the core hypothesis of this book. With the possible exception of Herodotus's Lydians, the hypothesis is certainly not old: eighty years ago the great economist F. Y. Edgeworth, who was in a position to know, proclaimed that the contrary thesis, that the marginal utility of income declines with each addition, was "universally admitted."[19] But how new is it? To my knowledge, I was publishing an original hypothesis when I wrote in 1986 that "between the level of income required for immediate survival and the level at which an individual is no longer unhappy for want of income, the marginal utility of income is typically *increasing,* and . . . it begins to diminish only above the point where it begins to yield some measure of positive satisfaction."[20]

But it appears that Bernard M. S. van Praag had proposed this hypothesis in a doctoral dissertation as early as 1968, which is to say, twenty-two years earlier. A bibliography of van Praag's work on this subject and of the work of his associates in the so-called Leyden School of economics may be found in an already-cited article by van Praag and Paul Frijters.[21] Interestingly, in this same article, van Praag and his fellow author seem to give precedence to F. G. van Herwaarden and A. Kapteyn, in a 1981 article.[22] In any case, the bibliography mentioned should enable those who are interested to settle the precedence issues definitively. The Leyden school based the hypothesis on data about people's perceptions of displeasing and pleasing incomes, mentioned earlier in this chapter.

In addition, thirty-eight years before my 1986 article Milton Friedman and L. J. Savage had advanced a similar hypothesis, which was known to me. They noted that people's common willingness to take certain risks could be rationalized by supposing that their marginal utility for income actually increased over a certain income range.[23] Their logic is reflected in our earlier discussion of the poor person who prefers the 50 percent risk of a ten-dollar parking ticket each day to the certainty of a five-dollar fee for parking legally: if marginal utility for income is rising, then the utility of bearing no cost for parking on half one's days, which leaves disposable funds undiminished on those days, and a ten-dollar cost on the other half will be greater than the utility of facing a five-dollar charge on all one's days.

But there are differences between Friedman's and Savage's position and mine with regard to specificity, evidence, and applications. Friedman and Savage did not equate the increasing marginal utility income range with poverty. So they failed to see that the hypothesis is further confirmed by its capacity to reconcile rationality with the whole set of behaviors that make up the poverty syndrome, including nonwork, dropping out of school, and failure to save. Furthermore, their case was weakened by the fact that they did not argue against *other* ways of rationalizing the existence of risk taking, besides their own hypothesis that the marginal utility of income is sometimes increasing. For instance, they did not dispute the alternative hypothesis that taking risks is simply one of the things rational people do when they feel an appetite for suspense and excitement. So even economists predisposed to see apparently irrational economic behavior as utility maximizing were not given a compelling reason to drop the long-accepted law of diminishing marginal utility.

Above all, because Friedman and Savage wrote within a positivistic paradigm that was intolerant of introspective evidence, they largely failed even to ask whether introspection supports the hypothesis of increasing marginal utility at certain income levels. So they overlooked the most powerful argument of all in support of their own hypothesis. Had they treated introspective evidence as legitimate in the first place, we can only guess whether they would have been able to think past the Epicurean Fallacy that misled so many of their predecessors in the prepositivistic period of economics.

Probably on account of this lack of specificity and compelling evidence, Friedman's and Savage's hypothesis did not catch on. I have found just two introductory economics texts that allude to the possibility that marginal utility of income rises before it falls, perhaps under the influence of Friedman and Savage, though it is not clear.[24] On the other hand, there are dozens that treat marginal utility as falling "from dollar one." In general, despite Friedman and Savage, introductory economics continues to assert the law of diminishing marginal utility.

The last difference between the Friedman and Savage theory and my theory is that they did not explore the implications of their hypothesis for allocation of resources among competing uses or for public policy regarding poverty. Perhaps the theoretical inquiry would have evolved much further if they or others had focused on its practical applications.

APPENDIX
The Case of Alfred Marshall

The economist Alfred Marshall (1842–1924) reached the conclusion that marginal utility always diminishes on the basis of an erroneous generalization from the marginal impact of pleasers, as outlined earlier. Marshall's version of the error deserves a closer look because he was so influential. One can watch Marshall getting into trouble as he reasons his way from his definition of "utility" to the staunch conclusion that "if we take a man as he is, without allowing time for any change in his character, the marginal utility of a thing to him diminishes steadily with every increase in his supply of it."[25] Step one is his prefatory comment that "utility is taken to be correlative to desire or want."[26] In the absence of any qualification, Marshall must mean that utility is correlative to desires or wants in general, regardless of their content. The relevance of this will be plain in a moment. Step two is his actual definition, that utility is the "fulfillment or satisfaction of . . . desire."[27] Up to this point, then, utility seems to be any satisfaction whatsoever. But here confusion begins. For "satisfaction" has two meanings. It has a wide sense, whereby any desire at all, be it for positive experience or relief, can be satisfied. But it also has a narrow sense, in which satisfaction is contrasted with relief of dissatisfaction.

To illustrate, in the first sense, one can say that someone with stings who desires salve and gets it has gotten satisfaction, but in the second sense the person is not even aiming for satisfaction, but only for relief of dissatisfaction. Now then, when Marshall says that "marginal utility diminishes," he must be thinking of utility as satisfaction in the second, narrower sense, that is, pleasure.[28] After all, there were bee stings and salves in Marshall's day as in ours, and their marginal impact would have been clear to anyone who cared to focus upon it. He must be thinking exclusively of pleasers, then. But Marshall's confidence that marginal utility *always* diminishes, that the law in question is a general one, must stem from thinking of utility as satisfaction in the broader sense — as what is gained when any desire at all is fulfilled. In short, Marshall reaches his incorrect conclusion because he equates utility with satisfaction and then equivocates on "satisfaction," relying on one meaning of the word to arrive at the idea of diminishing marginal utility and switching to the other meaning to argue that diminishing marginal utility is a universal law.

7

Policy

What Should We Do Differently If We Believe That
Marginal Utility Is Increasing Amid Scarcity?

I have now proposed and defended an account of some behaviors that
prolong and worsen poverty. In this chapter I explore some policy
implications. What should policymakers and others do to change
these behaviors if they accept what has been said up to this point?

As I have pointed out, the puzzles of poverty are basically two, one
about work and one about consumption smoothing. All of the behaviors I have discussed can be put in one (or both) of these categories. With respect to both categories, an important implication of my
theory for policy is that poverty-causing conduct on the part of poor
people is not self-limiting. For poverty itself lowers motivation to
work and to smooth consumption. But if failure to work and smooth
consumption are large factors in the prolongation and worsening of
poverty, then poverty is a self-prolonging and self-worsening human
condition. The poor may or may not always be with us, but their

condition will not go away by itself. This simple point has a world of practical implications for poverty policy, starting with the fact that society needs to have a poverty policy.

The silver lining, obviously, is that relieving poverty can initiate a virtuous cycle. Reducing poverty through transfers to the poor should tend to increase work and thereby to relieve poverty still further, and if transfers (or the effects of work) bring income to the level at which marginal utility begins to diminish, income smoothing to avert episodes of poverty likewise becomes efficient, making investment more attractive in the process. I hasten to add that this general approach does not entail unique strategies for changing each of the poverty-linked behaviors. Transfers to the poor may raise the likelihood of work, for instance, but there are many forms of transfer, including no-strings cash welfare and strategies to make work pay better, such as tax-based wage enhancements. I propose to go only a short distance into the advantages of one versus another because my priority is to explain why certain approaches will retain their value even as the details of the policy environment change.

Policies to Encourage Work

The policy implications of my hypothesis for the aim of promoting work are especially significant. They are significant because poor people's nonwork has a greater impact on their income than the other puzzling behaviors. The policy debate about how to achieve this aim in the United States and many other developed countries has taken on an air of Greek tragedy, in which equally noble public goals seem to be fundamentally opposed to each other. As we shall see, however, this opposition is an illusion.

The Helping Conundrum

The work debate in the United States and many other developed countries has been shaped by several assumptions. First is the belief that rich nations can and should relieve the poverty of their poor. Second, work and self-reliance are valuable, and everyone who can work and become self-reliant should do so. Third, the more material resources someone has, the less he will benefit from having still more. These three tenets generate what David Ellwood has called a "helping conundrum." For grant that the more income someone has, the less he will benefit from more. Then "when you give people money, food, or housing, you reduce the pressure on them to work and take care of themselves. No one seriously doubts this proposition."[1] This proposition entails that simply giving nonworking poor people money and other basic goods, which is the most reliable way of ensuring that their misery is relieved, is bound to threaten the goal of getting them to work. The shortest path to the first goal tends to take us further from the second goal. Conversely, society puts at risk the economic welfare of nonworking poor people if it tries to motivate them by minimizing the amount of no-strings help they receive — which is to say, minimizing assistance not contingent on work. For some people will not work even if they get no help when they do not work. What, then, is to be done?

One's stand on Ellwood's conundrum has become a litmus test of ideology. In the United States, conservatives and centrists insist that a policy of minimizing help to able-bodied people who do not help themselves is fair, practical, and aligned with American traditions. The policy is fair because it relieves the imposition on others who do work. Why should some people pull the wagon when others ride? It is practical because it tends to make people work, and work can relieve poverty in a large percentage of cases. And it is in the American tradition because it honors hard work and self-reliance. On the other hand, political liberals have attacked "tough love" policies as unjust for failing to respect the rights that poor people have just because they are human or, in another version, just because they are our compatriots. In this view, the very existence of misery, whether avoidable by the sufferer or not, creates a right to society's assistance. Alternatively, some liberals make the case for no-strings assistance by focusing not on the rights of recipients but on the virtue of being a donor. As a Dutch official said to me with pride (and a bit of condescension), "Here in the Netherlands, we love our losers." Further, liberals have attacked the tough love approach as misguided on the practical ground that motivating poor people toward self-sufficiency is useless if the opportunity to become self-sufficient is an illusion. Which, liberals say, it often is. After all, they point out, even tough love proponents do not claim that poverty would disappear entirely if every able-bodied person took an available job at the highest wage their education could command. Finally, as for American traditions, isn't bigheartedness as much an American tradition as self-reliance?

Undoubtedly the consensus on Ellwood's helping conundrum in the United States in recent years has been that the centrist and conservative position is correct. It is now widely felt that America went too far toward the "tender" pole of this conundrum during the War on Poverty of the sixties. Government undermined work with an unduly liberal welfare policy, and so we need to swing back in the "tough" direction, accepting that some people will have to go unhelped for the sake of strengthening the incentives of poor people to help themselves. The popularity of this view is evident in public approval of the 1996 welfare reforms — favored by 68 percent in the year they were passed.[2] For the 1996 reforms limited a poor adult's eligibility for no-strings cash assistance—that is, assistance not contingent upon involvement in the workforce—to a period of two years. After that, the recipient has to become involved in the workforce to continue getting welfare payments. Moreover, the reforms limited eligibility for any welfare payments to five years in a person's lifetime.[3] The toughening of public opinion can also be inferred from the fact that these reforms enjoyed bipartisan support in the Senate (though not in the House of Representatives, where 165 out of 195 Democrats opposed the bill), not to mention that they were signed into law by a Democratic president, albeit after he had vetoed two earlier versions of the legislation.[4]

Making Work Pay

But as if to mitigate the starkness of the helping conundrum and soften the hard choices it presents, yet another approach to motivation has gained strong support among policy thinkers and the public as well. This is "making work pay"—which is to say, making work pay better than it does in the labor market. This entails making work a more attractive option for low-income people through transfers and other provisions (for example, earned income disregards for cash welfare recipients and minimum wage laws) whose benefits depend on the recipient's working. Some of the economic assumptions behind this approach are not widely understood, but they are simple enough. To begin with, this approach accepts the conventional wisdom that marginal utility is everywhere diminishing. In other words, it accepts the proposition that for rich and poor alike getting a higher income from any source—be it an unconditional payment or an increase in hourly wage—will reduce the marginal utility of further dollars. Supposedly, then, an income increase will put a downward pressure on the number of hours that person will want to work. This is what economists call the income effect on motivation. But policymakers also believe, reasonably enough, that higher hourly wages will simultaneously put an *upward* pressure on the number of hours someone will want to work. This is known as the substitution effect. The existence of the substitution effect stands to reason, of course, because if my hourly wage goes from five dollars to ten, I give up twice as much by not working for one hour, which is bound to make an hour of leisure less attractive. What, then, determines whether a wage raise will increase or reduce the number of hours worked?

What the making work pay strategy assumes, specifically, is that as a matter of fact, while the income effect may be stronger than the substitution effect among rich people, the substitution effect is stronger than the income effect among poor people.[5] The two effects of a wage hike are vectors bearing on work motivation in opposed directions, in other words, and in the lower income ranges the upward pressure is stronger, while in the upper income ranges the downward pressure is stronger. In commonsense terms, giving an hourly raise to Jones will incline him to work more hours when he is poor and needs the extra money, but when Jones becomes rich and ceases to need extra money so badly, he will eventually use his wage raises to buy himself out of work and consume more leisure.[6] It is on the strength of this belief that current poverty policy in America not only shies away from unconditional help but positively favors wage subsidies as ways to help the poor.

The making work pay strategy underlies a number of specific federal and state policies and provisions. First, the reformed federal welfare system, which now varies from state to state, has maintained the previous practice of subsidizing the wages of welfare recipients who work, insofar as their welfare payments are reduced by less than 100 percent of their earnings in the labor market. In addition, some but not all states use their discretion to disregard a certain amount of earned income completely for a period of time in calculating the welfare benefits that recipients are allowed to keep. Further, making work pay underlies the federal Earned Income Tax Credit (EITC), which has grown into a more than thirty-eight-billion-dollar program since the 1996 welfare reform, more than twice the budget of the federal cash welfare program. As its name suggests, the EITC raises the incomes of low-income people if they are subject to taxation, which is to say, if they work for pay. A recent book on policies to help low-income workers describes the EITC as follows: "As an 'earnings credit,' it pays benefits to workers based on family size and earned income. In their phase-in range, EITC benefits increase with earned income, creating a positive work incentive for some recipients. Those who qualify may use the credit to offset federal tax liabilities, receive a lump sum payment as a tax refund, or apply to receive advance EITC payments in their paycheck."[7] Minimum wage laws and the relatively loose labor force participation requirements of the Food Stamp program are among the other policies designed to make work pay.

Beyond the Helping Conundrum

Before I try to assess the strategy of making work pay, let me go back for a moment to Ellwood's helping conundrum. Should we be "hard noses" who are prepared to let nonworkers go unhelped in order to preserve incentives for self-help? or should we be "bleeding hearts" who give nonworkers no-strings help, despite the fact that such a practice will make them less likely to help themselves? It should be evident that both sides of the debate collapse if letting poor nonworkers go unhelped does not preserve work incentives anyway. Neither the principle that helping should be sacrificed to preserving incentives nor the opposing principle that incentives should be sacrificed to helping is worth defending if the two things are not in tension in the first place. And they are not. For the belief that tough love motivates the poor rests on the assumption that income dulls the appetite for more income at all income levels. But on the contrary, the marginal utility of resources is rising amid true scarcity. Therefore the impact of small income increases on the number of hours a poor person will want to work at any given wage will be positive, not negative. Conversely, the impact of toughening welfare programs will be to reduce the number of hours the recipient will want to work.[8]

The underlying concept is illustrated by the story in chapter 5 about the poor worker and her six-mile walk to work. Recall that she does not consider it worth the effort to converse in French in exchange for a one-mile ride, because the relief she will get from having one fewer blister, one fewer unwashed dish, and one fewer reprimand is minor when she still has five miles to walk — and five blisters, dirty dishes, and reprimands still to endure. But when she has been given a five-mile ride, no strings attached, and there is only one mile left to walk, the same effort to converse in French becomes an acceptable price to pay for a one-mile ride. For the relief of having one fewer blister, unwashed dish, and reprimand when she has only one of each to begin with is not minor but significant. By the same token, if you have seven daily stings, and you have been getting one dab of salve, and suddenly you get five dabs of salve — never mind how, for the moment — the increase raises the benefit you stand to get from a next dab of salve. After all, the perceived difference between six unrelieved stings and five is a lot smaller than the perceived difference between two uncured stings and one. So the increase is bound to put positive pressure on your willingness to work for a next dab. Looking at it from the other side, those four extra dabs you have begun to get make the leisure you might enjoy by not working for a next dab of salve more expensive, as measured by the relief that is foregone, and this higher price of leisure is a discouragement.

In the absence of the helping conundrum, pragmatic conservatives and centrists have one fewer issue to disagree with liberals about. The choice between promoting the self-sufficiency of the poor and guaranteeing their well-being is doubtless an agonizing one. Fortunately, it is not a choice that needs to be made. The tragic quality of recent policy debates rests on a mistake. But while there is in this sense no helping conundrum amid *poverty,* the conundrum is very real above the level of sufficiency. Once resources rise past the level where they bring relief and begin to bring positive satisfaction, the law of diminishing marginal utility does properly apply. While each dab of salve makes the next dab more attractive, each portion of dessert makes the next portion less attractive. So in this above-sufficiency range there really is tension between helping and motivating for self-help. This makes it ironic that in the current political scene the tough love approach is so popular with middle-class people as a strategy for motivating the poor and so often overlooked as a remedy for motivating middle-class people themselves, seeing that it is likelier to work on middle-class people.

An intriguing exception to this ironic situation is the Old Money class within the broad category of the well-off. Many observers have noted that American families that have been wealthy for many generations are comparatively stingy with their children. This is evident in small matters like allowances. Likewise, daily life at the boarding schools to which Old Money families often send their children is generally spartan, even if the schools are expensive and their facilities are grand. There is a pattern of pushing the children "out of the nest" and onto their own at a comparatively young age. Even vacations are comparatively rugged, often being spent in cold-water spots like the Adirondacks or the coast of Maine. It is true that this toughness is partially symbolic. Inheritances typically await. Yet the patterns can be seen as efforts to motivate by depriving or at least not spoiling the children at an age when work habits are being formed, consistent with the law of diminishing marginal utility.[9]

The general principle of motivation that emerges here is well summarized in the adage, Comfort the afflicted and afflict the comfortable.[10] Graphically, the point can be made by turning back to figure 6.2. Policies that in effect move rich people or poor people from the flat (low marginal utility) regions at their respective extremes of the total utility function toward the middle levels of income should increase the motivation of both groups to work for marginal improvements in their income, precisely because it is in these middle regions that the utility function is steep. This is consistent with the common observation that in every society it is the truly middle classes that work hardest. The American founding father Richard Henry Lee was speaking for many when he said that the solid part of the community is "the men of middling property."[11]

Making Work Pay (Continued)

Where does all this leave the currently popular strategies that attempt to motivate low-income people to work by making work pay better? The first thing to note is that if the so-called income effect on work motivation really is positive rather than negative below sufficiency, then the usual rationale for strategies to make work pay is mistaken. For remember that the advantage of these strategies has seemed to be this: that while more income from any source depresses motivation by making work less necessary, strategies that enhance poor people's earnings push on their motivation in the opposite direction simultaneously by making work more worthwhile (the economists' substitution effect); and that the second effect is stronger than the first effect for poor people. But in reality, I contend, for poor people the income effect of an effective wage hike (such as is provided by the EITC) and the substitution effect of a wage hike push on motivation in the same direction, namely, upward. The substitution effect and the income effect will not be opposed but mutually reinforcing. To illustrate with our familiar image, suppose you suffer from seven stings a day, and your allotment of dabs of salve per day has risen from one to five. Suppose, too. that this has happened because you work for dabs of salve, and your dabs-per-hour wage rate has risen (perhaps on account of a government program of wage supplements). Then you have two reasons, not just one, to work more hours. First, it costs you more in dabs to take an hour off (the substitution effect), and second, marginal dabs themselves now bring more relief (the income effect). In sum, conventional economic assumptions lead us to underestimate the positive effect of programs like the EITC on work motivation.

Conversely, when effective wage rates fall for poor people, the negative effect on motivation will also be twofold: it becomes cheaper to buy oneself out of an hour of work, and the subjective benefit that would be derived from a marginal dollar is reduced at the same time. Going back to our image, if your pay in dabs of salve leaves you two dabs a day short of what you need, and your rate of pay falls to a point where you are six dabs short, then you give up less salve by taking an hour off, and a dab now does you less good anyway.

Seeing that the income effect and the substitution effect of strategies to make work pay will be mutually reinforcing, making work pay is a double-barreled antipoverty approach. By contrast, no-strings assistance is a single-barreled approach. For while it does have a positive income effect, still it lacks a positive substitution effect — which is to say, it costs no more to take an hour off when you have just been given some money. Yet it does not follow that making work pay should be society's sole strategy for motivating poor people to work, and that no-strings assistance has no role to play. For instance, consider nonworkers who have not been drawn into the workforce even by the prospect of supplemented wages. Assuming rationality, this must be because the marginal utility of those supplemented wages is still too low to attract them, given the burdens of the available jobs, their other pursuits, and their other income sources. One way to tip the balance in favor of working would be to increase the size of the wage supplement, perhaps by raising the funding of the EITC program. But my hypothesis suggests an alternative that may have advantages. That is to give nonworking poor people no-strings assistance. By raising the marginal utility of dollars, these grants should raise the attractiveness of the same supplemented wages that previously failed to draw recipients into the workforce, and it may tip the scales for a significant number, again without forcing changes in the EITC program itself. This might be advantageous if, for instance, the cost of operating a more generous EITC program turned out to be bigger than the cost of running a program of no-strings assistance for this purpose.

But whatever the advantages of the no-strings approach may be, many would argue that the practical reality of American politics is that no-strings public assistance of the old Aid to Families with Dependent Children type has become unthinkable. If that is true, then at the very least society should appreciate that the urgency of finding *other* ways to get nonworking poor people into the workforce is greater than it has seemed to be on conventional economic assumptions. Putting it the other way around, policymakers and the voting public, having anathematized no-strings assistance to the poor, should not be allowed to assuage any vestiges of liberal guilt with the thought that poverty itself will always function as the disincentive of last resort for voluntary nonwork. For reasons that should be clear by now, it won't. These other ways of getting poor people into the workforce might include relaxing prohibitions on gray-area enterprises.

A last point about the EITC program. I have already noted one way in which conventional economic assumptions tend to make us underestimate the positive effect of this program on the work motivation of poor people. Namely, conventional economics leads us to expect the income effect of the wage supplements on work motivation to be negative, whereas it is positive. A second way that conventional economics makes us underestimate the benefits of the EITC has to do with the limits that policymakers put on the supplements in order to control the cost of the program. What happens in the EITC is that net wages are enhanced by about 30 percent up to a certain level of earnings, but then, when the individual's subsidy hits a certain level, the subsidy does not grow further with increased earnings. Instead, it levels off. Then, as earnings pass a second threshold, the absolute amount of the subsidy actually declines, until at a certain earnings level the subsidy phases down to nothing. According to conventional theory of labor supply, based as it is on the mistaken assumption that the income effect of marginal dollars on the poor is to push downward on work motivation, the effect of the EITC program is actually negative once the first earnings threshold is reached. For as earnings rise above that point, some or all of the basic subsidy is still being received, supposedly pushing down on motivation via the income effect, but the program is no longer raising the price of leisure by enhancing the hourly wage rate. By contrast, my theory predicts that even without a positive substitution effect, the program will continue to increase work motivation by raising income, up to its phase-out point.

Turning briefly from public policy to the problems of the private sector, one can notice another advantage of relying on the income effect rather than on the substitution effect. Consider, for instance, the employee retention problem that plagues the fast food industry. Here the need of each firm to remain competitive and profitable discourages it from providing incentives to workers by raising effective wage rates. An alternative approach might be to rely to a greater degree upon the positive income effect that exists (I have argued) among low-income people by focusing recruitment efforts on the least poor of the poor. In fact, many fast food chains do this already, insofar as they recruit retirees, who more often than younger prospects have savings, houses, and other wealth. Such employees in effect start with more dabs of salve and can therefore be expected to place a greater value on the very same earned income that fails to motivate younger workers over the long term.

A last, related issue concerns the shaping of public opinion. Opinion leaders in the United States and other advanced industrial nations have often been warned against casting the objective conditions of the poor in a positive light, for instance, by comparing them with worse conditions elsewhere in the world. The fear is that putting a positive spin on people's economic circumstances will tend to reduce the pressure for improvement. In light of my hypothesis I can partly agree and partly disagree. Suppose it were possible to move poor people from a state of misery to a state of high satisfaction by means of rhetoric, without changing their objective conditions. Doubtless that would lessen their eagerness to see their situation made better, whether through political change or their own work or some other means. But equally, getting people to see adverse circumstances as very, very bad could have the same effect. For, as we noted in the last chapter, the person who sees an income of twenty thousand dollars as two stings will be more likely to exert himself to improve it a little than someone who sees an income of twenty thousand dollars as six stings. For how much energy is it worth to go from six stings to five?

These considerations cast an interesting light on recent history. Thirty-five years ago the speeches and writings of American civil rights leaders often framed or interpreted the circumstances of their audiences by "comparing them up" — that is, measuring them against the circumstances of the middle classes and the upper middle classes or even against the images of the good life found within the American Dream. This was openly done for the sake of energizing audiences with discontent. The goal was reasonable enough, but according to my theory the strategy was probably counterproductive. For on my hypothesis any discontent that was added by the speeches would have *deenergized* audiences — by reducing the marginal relief to be expected from a small improvement in objective circumstances. It might even be argued that this rhetoric worsened the poverty problem it was meant to help relieve.

I shall not explore public policies to limit alcohol abuse here, because the medical and psychiatric issues would take the argument too far afield. But it is plausible to suppose that for a significant fraction of the population, the temptation to drink in quantity is a constant, held in check by the desire for income and the resulting need to work. (One is reminded of the tavern witticism, "Work is the curse of the drinking glass.") This is reflected in the fact that many people who drink at all drink much more while on vacation. But if so, then whatever raises the appreciation of income itself and of work on the part of low-income people can be expected to affect the disposition to binge when drinking alcohol.

Policies to Encourage School Persistence

For present purposes, schoolwork can be seen as a kind of work, one whose financial rewards are received indirectly in the form of higher pay for later efforts in the regular workplace. To this extent, the foregoing discussion of work is applicable to the problem of school persistence as well. Just as the low marginal utility of consumption that goes with poverty makes it satisfaction-efficient for many poor people not to work for pay, so the same factor makes it efficient for many poor young people not to work at building their later earning power by staying in school. Poor young people often understand that the financial rewards of school persistence on their part will yield them so little felt relief, owing to their financial condition itself, that school persistence is not worth the effort. Thus we have a vicious cycle, whereby poverty leads to dropping out, which prolongs poverty. But there is plainly an opportunity to replace it with a virtuous one. Anything that increases income, and thereby the marginal utility of earnings, raises the benefits of learning — since learning amplifies the financial rewards of later work. Hence reducing poverty should increase school persistence, which in turn should increase income. If this seems obvious by now, remember that on the conventional wisdom, low income elevates rather than depresses the marginal value of income, and so poor children's failure to persist in school appears to be costly instead of sensible in terms of long-run satisfaction. So costly, in fact, that its occurrence demands to be explained by postulating imprudence, or else lack of educational opportunity, unusual distaste for learning, or perverse public policy. Such explanations have sent policymakers in various unproductive directions. My account does not depend on any of those postulates, although it leaves room for some of them.

Policy to improve persistence should build on the account of dropping out that I have proposed. Capitalizing on the virtuous cycle just outlined by strengthening general antipoverty efforts is likely to be effective. A second worthy, if elusive, goal is raising the financial return on poor students' investment of time in school, understanding that a higher return may be necessary to retain poor students than nonpoor students. On the other hand, Aesopian jawboning about the prudence of staying in school is likely to be ineffective with low-income students because many or most students who decide to quit are choosing efficiently to begin with. The postulate of hostility to studying hard on the part of certain minority cultures seems unlikely to lead to helpful policy either. Atypical or deviant values do not explain the problematic patterns any better than imprudence does. (Here I hasten to add that in minimizing the importance of culture as a freestanding variable in attrition I do not mean to deny that cultural norms may play an important role by making individuals feel poorer or less poor at a given objective income, which may well affect behavior for reasons suggested in chapter 6.) Last, given the increase in per student expenditures in the United States in recent decades, the burden of proof rests squarely on those who would improve the persistence of poor students by improving their educational opportunities, however strong the equity arguments may be for action to reduce discrepancies created by differences in local funding.

A second aspect of the challenge of improving school persistence starts with a point made earlier: that education is an investment whose rewards tend to flow back smoothly over time, along with the earned income it enhances. But smooth consumption below sufficiency is wasteful. To that extent, the economic appeal of school as an investment will be reduced for low-income young people. This argues, as I said, for offering low-income students a significant amount of career-phase-specific training, notwithstanding the difficulties of tailoring curriculum to the needs of a particular industry. But as the virtuous cycle continues, new generations of a formerly poor family will eventually enter school entirely unburdened by poverty, so that consumption smoothing will be efficient, removing that barrier to persistence as well.

Postsecondary education too has big potential effects on future income, and policy should therefore aim to increase participation by students from low-income families. Given increasing marginal utility, telescoping the period of payout and telescoping the period of payback may be useful. In other words, the subjective investment represented by staying on in school past high school will be improved if the out-of-pocket and opportunity costs of a program are concentrated, since the pain inflicted by a given cost will be less if it is sustained in one year than if it is spread out over three or four. Likewise the subjective investment will be improved if the total payback is concentrated in a single phase of the prospective student's career, and in this sense there is probably wisdom in the practice of marketing job-specific educational programs to lower-income students, while aiming programs that purport to prepare someone for "a career, not just a job" at middle-class students.

Policies to Encourage Saving

Society at large wants to promote saving for a rainy day by low-income people for several reasons. First, their rainy days are very miserable. But, second, if poor people do not save, society will be obliged to provide them extra help from its own pocket on the rainy days. Finally, savings can be invested, thus offering the possibility of overcoming poverty entirely over time.

Ignore for a moment the fact that saved money can be invested so as to yield interest and capital appreciation. Leaving this aside, policy needs to recognize that not saving by low-income people can achieve a rational purpose, given variability of income. That purpose is allowing consumption itself to vary, which will maximize the relief derived from total income. When people who have nothing but rainy days fail to save for their very rainiest days, those days are going to be days of deep poverty. But there are worse things than having some days of deep poverty. For instance, there is having twice that many days on which the poverty is half as deep. That again is the point of Lydian prudence. Hence when poor people fail to save for their rainiest days, they may be doing what is best for themselves, or least bad, given their immediate options. This goes against the conventional wisdom, of course. Essentially the same point applies to the notion that poor people would be better off if they saved because they would then be better protected against the downside of economic risks.[12] On the contrary, rational poor people often do not save partly because they want the risks they take, which are many, to create ups and downs in their consumption.

Figuring in the opportunity to grow total income by investing the saved money plainly changes the analysis. This can make saving rational for low-income people. But efforts by policymakers to promote saving by providing an attractive return on the invested money must start with the recognition that it will take a significant return to induce a rational low-income person to smooth consumption — significant enough to outweigh what would otherwise be the irrationality of that pattern of consumption. To appreciate this more fully, recall from chapter 5 the case of the employer who is bewildered at the size of the bonus that is required to induce employees to spread their ten-month supply of transportation vouchers over twelve months.

From this standpoint, the failure of tax exemptions to motivate low- and middle-income people to contribute significantly to IRAs and 401(k)s should not be surprising. Since these households are in lower tax brackets, their tax exemptions for contributing a given sum to a retirement plan are lower, and the after-tax costs of contributing a given sum to a retirement plan are actually higher than for high-bracket households. Thus it costs someone with a 10 percent tax rate ninety dollars to contribute one hundred dollars to an IRA, while it costs a higher-income person with a 20 percent tax rate only eighty dollars. Everything else being equal, the lower-income saver's investments have a lower effective rate of return. On the other hand, there seems to be promise in the federal Saver's Credit program, legislated in 2001, since it provides a tax incentive for retirement saving that is *inversely* related to income. Roughly, the lower your income, the bigger your tax break for a given contribution. This still-small program is surely a step in the right direction because it responds to the fact that a bigger incentive will be needed to attract a poor person into a retirement saving plan than to attract a nonpoor person, given the countervailing force of consumption smoothing.[13] Strong returns for a family in one generation, made possible by a subsidized program like this, can do something to reduce the need for special incentives in future generations by helping raise family fortunes to the point where the consumption-smoothing motive and the investment motive for saving are aligned.

Besides improving the rate of return, another policy option for increasing savings for investment by low-income households would be to concentrate both the pay-in and the pay-out into shorter periods of time. For given increasing marginal utility, the pay-in will "hurt" less if it is gotten over with quickly than if it is drawn out, while the pay-out will bring more relief if concentrated than it will if it is drawn out. The government might experiment with lump-sum payouts of Social Security, for instance. This point parallels what was said earlier about the educational investment in human capital.

Policies to Discourage Crime

Much of what has been said about saving can be said about crime. The behavior of low-income criminals, like that of low-income nonsavers, can be rationalized by seeing it as sacrificing some potential income to get the benefits of uneven consumption, in this case owing to episodes of incarceration. From this perspective, increasing the differential between the income gained from crime and that gained from honest work — by raising the odds of punishment, lengthening sentences, or making (honest) work pay better — is likelier to be effective than strategies built on the assumption that criminals are dysfunctional and hence unresponsive to sticks and carrots of this kind. Increasing the crime–work differential is also likelier to be effective than strategies built on the assumption of atypical preferences. In addition, any effective antipoverty policy should reduce crime by making consumption smoothing efficient, which means that politically speaking the public's antipathy to crime can be honestly harnessed in support of general public spending to relieve poverty.

8

Economic Justice Reconsidered

Two conceptions of economic justice pervade the thinking and practice of the industrialized democracies. On one conception, people are entitled to whatever goods they can produce themselves or get by trading their products for goods created by others. For instance, I am entitled to the vegetables I can grow myself, and I am entitled to whatever articles of clothing my neighbor has made and is willing to trade me for some of my vegetables. This understanding of economic justice honors self-reliance, autonomy, and free exchange. It does not honor effort or need directly. Someone who works very hard to write a novel that his neighbor does not want to read is not entitled to some of the clothes his neighbor has made just because he worked hard on his novel or just because he needs clothes. Rather his neighbor retains a natural right to keep or trade, or for that matter give away, all of the clothes he has made. Of course the neighbor may feel a moral obligation to give the needy novelist clothing, but on this conception the neighbor is not required to do so as a matter of justice. And correlative with each person's right to keep, trade, or give away his product is a right of the recipient, including his heirs, to keep, trade, or give it in turn. Proponents of this conception generally qualify it by granting that the group may coercively tax everyone to pay for generally valued goods that benefit people whether they contribute some of their own product or not. An example would be national defense. For without taxation everyone would want to benefit without paying, and these so-called public goods would not be provided at all.

The second popular idea of economic justice is that an allocation is just when it is proportional to individuals' needs: in the familiar phrase, "To each according to his needs." Both Marx and Lenin used this slogan, which had been introduced by the French socialist Louis Blanc in 1840, but its appeal extends beyond the traditional left. Who has not been struck by the injustice of a world in which some people have much more than they need, while others have much less? The appeal of need-proportional justice is strengthened by the consideration that the special talent and intelligence which help make some people wealthy in systems based on free exchange are themselves the undeserved results of a genetic lottery. Even the energy and ambition that are rewarded by the market may have much to do with the luck of the draw. Phil Ochs's line, "There but for fortune go you or I" is a powerful antidote to the sense of entitlement.

These two conceptions of justice appeal to modern people so powerfully that all industrialized economies are influenced by both. But various nations strike different balances between them. Those nations in which the commitment to need-proportional justice is relatively strong are commonly thought of as more socialistic, while those nations more influenced by the free-exchange understanding of economic justice are seen as more capitalistic. Sweden would be an example of the former, while the United States would be an example of the latter.

Is there any objective way to determine the proper balance between these rival conceptions of economic justice, or do we have to rely completely on the relative strength of our intuitions? One way forward is suggested by David Hume's assertion in his famous treatise of 1739 that justice is accepted as a norm because and to the extent that it enhances the general welfare.[1] This idea is supported by the consideration that any norm that was socially destructive would have long since been borne down in the ruins of the society that embraced it. Hume's idea suggests that we might discover an optimal balance between the two conceptions of justice by comparing the social utility of various balances between them.

Thus we might start with pretax incomes, as an approximation of allocation based on free exchange. On the usual view, respecting such a pattern tends to promote social utility because work incentives — the hope of being rewarded for productivity and the fear of being made destitute on account of not contributing — enlarge the social product; and the bigger the pie, everything else being equal, the greater the well-being of society. On the other hand, by honoring need-justice and transferring income from higher earners to lower earners, governments can contribute to aggregate utility also, since (on the usual view) the marginal utility of a dollar is greater for those who have fewer dollars than for those who have more dollars.

Implicit here is that giving weight to needs by transferring market-allocated income from those with higher incomes to those with lower incomes poses a dilemma. It has two contrary effects. It exerts not only a positive pressure on aggregate utility but a countervailing, negative pressure on aggregate utility, since the transfers will undermine work incentives, shrinking the social product. People are less likely to work hard if they know their wages are going to be reduced for the benefit of others, and they are less likely to avoid idleness if they know that the natural consequences of idleness are going to be softened by transfers from the rich. Or so it would seem. Interestingly, Jeremy Bentham, who was the first to articulate the utilitarian argument for need-based justice, spotted this problem immediately, and this led him to reject need-based transfers. He strongly, indeed almost hysterically, opposed complete income equalization as follows: "To maximization of happiness would be substituted universal annihilation in the first place of happiness — in the next place of existence. Evil of the second order, — annihilation of happiness by the universality of the alarm, and the swelling of the danger into certainty: Evil of the third order, — annihilation of existence by the certainty of the non-enjoyment of the fruit of labour, and thence the extinction of all inducement to labour."[2]

Faced with these countervailing impacts on aggregate utility, the utilitarian solution to the balance problem seems simple enough in principle. One gauges the impact on social well-being of each small deviation from market-set incomes in the direction of need-proportionality. The question at each step is whether the addition to aggregate utility from redistributing dollars toward those with lower incomes and thus higher marginal utility is bigger than the loss of aggregate utility caused by the weakening of work incentives. As long as the net impact on aggregate utility is positive, one continues to make the transfers, stopping only when the negative effects begin to outweigh the positive. The project is neatly summarized by Richard Layard as follows: "So we should tax the rich for the benefit of the poor. But as we do this, we blunt the incentives facing both rich and poor. Thus as we raise the tax rate, the total size of the cake falls. . . .

The optimum is where the gains from further redistribution are just outweighed by the losses from the shrinking of the cake."[3]

This seems plausible enough. But as we shall see in this chapter, the hypothesis of this book—that marginal utility rises amid scarcity—has drastic implications for this approach to the balancing problem.

Before looking at points of disagreement, however, let me note an important point of agreement between my theory and the usual utilitarian analysis. The version of my hypothesis that I defended in chapter 6 entails that, *leaving aside incentive (pie-shrinking) effects,* direct transfers from the nonpoor to the poor that relieve poverty will increase the welfare of society. This conclusion is entirely consistent with the conclusion utilitarians have drawn since Bentham. Thus consider figure 6.2. For simplicity, suppose first a society composed of two equally large classes. A poor class lives in poverty at income A, which is to say, BA dollars below sufficiency, while a nonpoor class lives at C, which is to say, BC dollars above sufficiency. If BC is transferred to the poor class, so that both groups end up at sufficiency, the utility gain to the formerly poor, namely, the relief of misery AE, is greater than the utility loss to those who formerly lived at a more than sufficient level, namely, the loss of positive satisfaction DC. This is not an arbitrary result of gratuitous assumptions about the utility function. Rather, it must be so if we hypothesize a uniform utility function that (a) reflects introspected experience, (b) rationalizes the ancient prohibition against splurge-skimp consumption, and (c) rationalizes the uneven consumption so common among the truly needy in all eras. In other words, one does not have to assume that marginal utility diminishes at all income levels to reach the conclusion that (ignoring incentive effects) eliminating poverty through transfers from the nonpoor will produce a net gain in social well-being.

Turning from this simplified, two-class model to the reality of the contemporary United States, the utility gains from eliminating poverty by direct transfers could be much greater. For, of course, it would not be necessary to level down the income of the group just above sufficiency in order to eliminate poverty. The aggregate income of the top quintile, which starts at about eighty-three thousand dollars a year, amounts to just over half of all income earned, while the aggregate income of the bottom quintile, which ends in the neighborhood of the poverty line at about eighteen thousand dollars, amounts to about one-thirtieth of all income earned.[4] (The following image may be helpful. If all the income earned in the United States were represented by a one-pound steak, and the quintiles were five individuals, the top consumer would be eating eight ounces of steak, while the bottom consumer would be eating just over half an ounce.) Thus one way to double the income of the bottom quintile, ending almost all poverty by standard measures, would be for government to tax the top quintile 6 percent and transfer the money. (I will ignore the leaky bucket problem and other complications for clarity.) The loss in positive experience that the top quintile would suffer from giving up 6 percent of its income (a half an ounce from its half-pound of steak) would be much less than in the earlier example, and so the net gain in aggregate utility would be much greater.

A second point of agreement with the usual utilitarian analysis is that there would be immediate utility gains from transferring funds down within the nonpoor part of the population, for instance, transferring ten thousand dollars from each billionaire to a household with an annual income of one hundred thousand dollars. This should be evident from the fact that on my hypothesis marginal utility is diminishing above sufficiency, as per the usual view. It is not clear whether this should count as a utilitarian argument in favor of need-proportional justice, however, because it is not clear whether the one-hundred-thousand-dollar household can be said to *need* ten thousand dollars more, however much it may want ten thousand dollars and stand to benefit from it.

This brings me to several points of difference between the usual utilitarian analysis and my own. To see the first difference, suppose we ask the question whether, supposing a fixed pie, income ought to be transferred down, not from the rich to the poor and not within the class of the rich, but from the moderately poor people (or those living just at the poverty line) to the very poor people. This might be a practical question in a nation that was, as a whole, very poor, and that was not receiving help from richer nations. Need-proportional justice would say yes because the very poor have a greater need for income than the moderately poor. "To each according to his need" would call for a downward transfer, even among the poor. But on my hypothesis — and still ignoring incentive effects and assuming a fixed pie — the answer would be no.

This can be justified by going back to the example of the six-mile walk to work. Suppose there are a hundred people who live at this distance from their work, and that market factors have resulted in an allocation of full bus fare to fifty of these people and no bus fare at all to the other fifty. And suppose there are no rich people with cars to provide a resource-side solution. Would taxing away half the bus fare of those who have bus fare and redistributing it to those who do not have it raise the well-being of the group? On the contrary, this would lower the aggregate well-being of the group because, again, three blisters, three unwashed dishes, and three reprimands are more than half as burdensome as six. This means that the relief felt by two people who still have to walk three miles each is less than the relief of one person who gets to ride all the way. (If this is not intuitive, start by asking yourself whether it would make sense to redistribute the bus fare if the tribulations of a three-mile walk were equal to those of a six-mile walk, and then change the supposition so that the tribulations of three are just a tiny bit less than those of six, and so on.)

This result may help us make sense of two striking facts. First is the relationship that seems to hold between the stage of a country's economic development and the degree of its income equality. The consensus among development economists supports a hypothesis offered by Simon Kuznets fifty years ago, which says in part that "when GNP reaches a level characteristic of industrial economies, the distribution of income may then become more equal."[5] Why should this be the case? If my own hypothesis is correct, then perhaps preindustrial societies tolerate a great deal of income inequality because redistribution policies that would cause everyone to skimp more equally would reduce aggregate relief, as compared with allowing a pattern in which some people skimp a little while others skimp a lot. (The analogy to Lydian prudence will be obvious.) But later in the course of a country's development, when industrialization creates the possibility of leveling everyone's income at sufficiency or higher, people appreciate that transfers from better-off to worse-off people would yield at least short-run gains in aggregate utility. This recognition produces social pressure for a degree of income equality that had not previously been efficient. The second striking fact that my hypothesis seems to make sense of is the very late historical appearance of need-proportional economic equality as an ethical ideal. While political and religious equality are old notions, the ideal of economic equality seems to be no older than the Industrial Revolution. I suggest this can be rationalized by the hypothesis that skimp-a-little/skimp-a-lot distribution is efficient amid scarcity and equality is efficient amid plenty, when taken together with the fact that the Industrial Revolution itself created enough wealth to offset poverty for the first time in history.[6]

A critic might object at this point that our utility function could be used to justify putting the least poor of the poor people ahead of the very poorest people in distributing assistance, since the very poorest people, by reason of their poverty itself, are the least efficient at extracting relief from a given quantity of resources. Putting the least poor of the poor ahead of the poorest is sharply at odds with "to each according to his needs" and with many people's intuitions. But granting that this probably feels wrong to you, perhaps moral feelings are an untrustworthy guide here. For one thing, most of the allocations that you and I make are allocations among nonpoor, nondeprived claimants, and *among the nondeprived* the least well-off claimant does normally have the highest marginal utility. At least this is true according to the function I have proposed in this book. Perhaps, then, we should not trust our feelings in a kind of case so different from the familiar type. Second, what would feel *really* right, to me at least, is relieving poverty in America completely — transferring half an ounce from those with half a pound. But given that that option is politically impossible, maybe the suboptimal choices, such as the choice of which poor people should get the tenth of an ounce that is in fact being transferred, are simply confusing to moral common sense.

This brings me to the deferred question of incentives. Predictably, I think the usual utilitarian approach to balancing the two conceptions of justice goes seriously wrong over incentives. As you recall, the usual view assumes that transfers from the rich to the poor honoring need-proportional justice will shrink the pie by harming the work incentives of both donors and recipients. One objection to this that has nothing specifically to do with my theory stems from the textbook doctrine that as wages rise, more and more labor will be supplied, up to a point, but then the supply curve of labor bends backward. A point is reached eventually where earners want more leisure more than more money. But if so, then for the well-paid people in question, net wage reductions on account of increased earnings taxes should actually increase the number of hours they work, at least until wages fall to the point where wages and hours worked are positively correlated. The tax makes their leisure cheaper, but their income is so much lower that they feel they have to give up some of their leisure anyway.[7] Thus, up to a point, the social product pie should tend to grow, not shrink, as a result of taxing the rich to give to the poor. This consideration should weaken the appeal of market-defined justice to those who care about maximizing the overall well-being of society.

Moreover, the standard utilitarian view, that transfers are bound to shrink the pie, seems clearly wrong when we turn from transfers' effects on the motivations of rich donors to transfers' effects on the motivations of poor recipients. For, as I have repeatedly argued, the normal effect of small transfers on a recipient who is poor will be to increase the relief that he or she derives from the next dollar — and thus the appeal of the work needed to get that dollar. So here again transfers should increase rather than shrink the social product. The caution is that the transfers must not be so generous that recipients are raised above sufficiency, in which case their effects on work motivation will indeed be to dampen it.[8] And as for the form of the transfer, work should be made more attractive even if the transfer takes the form of a no-strings grant, and not only if it comes as a wage enhancement.

The original notion was that we can find the optimal balance between need-proportional justice and market-defined justice in an economic system by finding the point where utility gains from incremental transfers downward, away from the market-set income allocation, are outweighed by utility losses. This notion has now been qualified almost beyond recognition. For it emerges that not all downward transfers will wring more utility from transferred dollars even in the short run. This is true, for instance, in situations of aggregate shortage. Moreover, it has emerged that not all need-driven transfers put downward pressure on utility by weakening work incentives and shrinking the pie. A striking illustration of the latter point would be small transfers from the very well-off in the United States to the working poor in the form of wage supplements. Such transfers can be expected to wring extra utility from the transferred dollars themselves, while at the same time increasing the work-motivation of both the well-off donors and the poor recipients, on whom there is exerted both a positive income effect and a positive substitution effect. There is no utility trade-off in sight here. The agonizing dilemma, whereby social utility gains from small transfers to the poor are supposedly offset by social utility losses, turns out to be an illusion. The practical upshot in the particular case of the United States is surely that the optimum balance between need-justice and market-defined justice is closer to pure need-justice than is generally appreciated.

Notes

1. What Poverty Is

1. Greg J. Duncan et al., *Years of Poverty, Years of Plenty: The Changing Economic Fortunes of American Workers and Families* (Ann Arbor: Survey Research Center, Institute for Social Research, University of Michigan, 1984), 45.

2. I am indebted for information about Micronesia to my son Oliver, who lived on the tiny island of Unanu in Chuuk State from September 2001 until June 2002.

3. Mickey Kaus, *The End of Equality* (New York: Basic Books, 1992).

4. Charles Murray, *In Pursuit: Of Happiness and Good Government* (New York: Simon and Schuster, 1988), 73–82.

5. Bradley R. Schiller, *The Economics of Poverty and Discrimination,* 9th ed. (Upper Saddle River, N.J.: Pearson Prentice Hall, 2004), 40–41; for other thought experiments of this type, though with a different point, see Murray, *In Pursuit,* 73–82.

6. U.S. Bureau of the Census, "Poverty Thresholds for 2005 by Size of Family and Number of Related Children Under 18 Years," last revised Au-

gust 29, 2006. http://www.census.gov/hhes/poverty/threshld/thresh
05.html.

7. See, for instance, John Iceland, *Poverty in America: A Handbook* (Berkeley: University of California Press, 2006).

8. Ibid., 35.

2. Behavioral Factors in Poverty

1. Joel Schwartz, *Fighting Poverty with Virtue: Moral Reform and America's Urban Poor, 1825–2000* (Bloomington: Indiana University Press, 2000), 18.

2. Ibid., 6, 17.

3. Oscar Lewis, *La Vida: A Puerto Rican Family in the Culture of Poverty—San Juan and New York* (New York: Random House, 1966).

4. Later we shall take one more step and argue that whether the poverty line is low or high in a given setting, not only the causes of that so-called poverty but also the *causes of the behaviors that help cause that poverty* tend to be the same. In short, some of the deepest roots of poverty are the same regardless of what material condition we identify as impoverished.

5. U.S. Bureau of the Census, 2000 data, cited in Schiller, *Economics,* 79.

6. Bernadette D. Proctor and Joseph Dalaker, *Poverty in the United States: 2002,* U.S. Bureau of the Census (September 2003), 8; This is consistent with international data. See Rosa Martínez, Jesús Ruiz-Huerta, and Luis Ayala, "The Contribution of Unemployment to Inequality and Poverty in OECD Countries," *Economics of Transition* 9, no. 2 (July 2001): 10–12.

7. Ron Haskins and Isabel Sawhill, "Work and Marriage: The Way to End Poverty and Welfare," Brookings Institution Policy Brief (Washington: Brookings Institution, September 2003), 3.

8. National Center for Educational Statistics, "Elementary and Secondary Education," in *Digest of Educational Statistics, 2004* (March 2005), table 108, http://nces.ed.gov/programs/digest/d04/tables/dt04_108.asp.

9. U.S. Bureau of the Census, 2000 data, cited in Schiller, *Economics,* 157.

10. Duncan, *Years of Poverty, Years of Plenty,* 110–11.

11. An exception is Marianne Bertrand, Sendil Mullainathan, and Eldar Shafir, "Behavioral Economics and Marketing in Aid of Decision Making Among the Poor," *Journal of Public Policy and Marketing* 25, no. 1 (Spring 2006): 8–23.

12. Duncan, *Years of Poverty, Years of Plenty,* 40–43. Evidently the likelihood of

dropping into poverty grew in the 1990s. See Mark R. Rank, Daniel A. Sandoval, and Thomas A. Hirschl, "The Increase of Poverty Risk and Income Insecurity in the U.S. Since the 1970s," presentation given at the American Sociological Association 2004 Annual Meeting, Section on Sociology of Population Paper Session: The Demography of Poverty, abstract found online at http://convention.allacademic.com/asa2004/view_paper_info.html?pub_id=2759&part_id1=24792.

13. Susan Dynarski and Jonathan Gruber, "Can Families Smooth Variable Earnings?" in *Brookings Papers on Economic Activity 1997:1, Macroeconomics,* ed. William C. Brainard and George L. Perry, 229–303 (Washington: Brookings Institution Press, 1997).

14. Brian K. Bucks, Arthur B. Kennickell, and Kevin B. Moore, "Recent Changes in U.S. Family Finances: Evidence from the 2001 and 2004 Survey of Consumer Finances," *Federal Reserve Bulletin* (2006), A5, http://www.federalreserve.gov/pubs/bulletin/2006/financesurvey.pdf.

15. Dynarski and Gruber, "Variable Earnings," 272.

16. Mary Kay Fox and Nancy Cole, "Health-Related Risks from Nutrition and Health Characteristics of Low-Income Populations," in *Nutrition and Health Characteristics of Low-Income Populations:* vol. 1, *Food Stamp Program Participants and Nonparticipants,* Economic Research Service, U.S. Department of Agriculture (December 2004), 64–65. Also available at www.ers.usda.gov/publications/efan04014-1/. Other researchers agree that "poverty can . . . increase the propensity to use substances." R. Lorraine Collins and Mariela C. Shirly, "Vulnerability to Substance Use Disorders in Adulthood," in *Vulnerability to Psychopathology: Risk Across the Lifespan,* ed. Rick E. Ingram and Joseph M. Price, 151 (New York: Guilford Press, 2001).

17. Dale Heien, "The Relation between Alcohol Consumption and Earnings," *Journal of Studies on Alcohol* (September 1996): 540.

18. NPR/Kaiser/Kennedy School Poll (2001), section II, question 9, http://www.npr.org/programs/specials/poll/poverty/staticresults.html.

19. W. Kip Viscusi, *Smoking: Making the Risky Decision* (New York: Oxford University Press, 1992), 111; James P. Smith, "Healthy Bodies and Thick Wallets: The Dual Relation between Health and Economic Status," *Journal of Economic Perspectives* 13 (Spring 1999): 145–66; U.S. Bureau of the Census, Current Population Survey (March 2001), cited in Schiller, *Economics,* 121; NPR/Kaiser/Kennedy School Poll, section II, question 8.

20. Morgan Kelly, "Inequality and Crime," *Review of Economics and Statistics* 82, no. 4 (2000): 530–39.

21. James Q. Wilson and Allan Abrahamse, "Does Crime Pay?" *Justice Quarterly* 9, no. 3 (September 1992): 359–77; U.S. Bureau of the Census, Housing and Household Economic Statistics Division, "Historical Poverty Tables — Poverty by Definition of Income," last revised December 14, 2005, http://www.census.gov/hhes/www/poverty/histpov/rdp01.html.

22. Wilson and Abrahamse, "Does Crime Pay?" 370.

23. Haskins and Sawhill, "Work and Marriage," 1.

3. Some Theories

1. The taxonomy of theories of poverty in this chapter has much in common with the taxonomies in Schiller, *Economics,* and in Lawrence Mead, *The New Politics of Poverty: The Nonworking Poor in America* (New York: Basic Books, 1992). One difference between mine and Schiller's is that he treats what he (and I) calls the restricted opportunity theory sometimes as an explanation of nonwork and sometimes as an explanation of poverty despite work. Since my taxonomy categorizes theories of behavior only, I treat the restricted opportunity theory only as an explanation of nonwork. Another difference is that Schiller's taxonomy apparently does not include the theory that poverty-sustaining behavior is irrational and self-defeating. For him, evidently, all choices not affected by restricted opportunity or bad public policy are rational. See Schiller, *Economics,* 5. Mead's taxonomy differs from mine too. Mead does not put explanations of nonwork that postulate that nonworkers put an unusual priority on non-material goods (leisure, child care) into the category of efforts to "rationalize" nonwork. For him, not working because one prioritizes non-material goods cannot be called rational because calling such a thing rational would supposedly force us into the absurdity that any and all behavior is rational. See Mead, *New Politics,* 134–36. By contrast, I categorize what I call the atypical preference theory as an effort to rationalize the behavior of the poor.

2. One observer who blames poverty on the dysfunctions of the poor was Edward Banfield: "The lower-class person lives from moment to moment, he is unable or unwilling to take into account the future or to control his impulses . . . being improvident and irresponsible, he is likely

also to be unskilled, to move frequently from one dead-end job to another, to be a poor husband and father." *The Unheavenly City: The Nature and Future of Our Urban Crisis* (Boston: Little, Brown, 1970), quoted in Iceland, *Poverty in America,* 95. More recently, similar weaknesses have been imputed to people generally (not just the poor) by the school of economics known as behavioralism. As one periodical summarizes, behavioralism says that "because of ignorance or intemperance, lack of will-power or brainpower, people choose badly . . . fail to exercise their choices in their own best interest." "The New Paternalism," *The Economist,* April 8–14, 2006, 67.

3. *New Politics,* 136.

4. For applications of this approach to working and workplace effectiveness, see JoAnn Prause et al., "Favourable Employment Status Change and Psychological Depression," *Applied Psychology* 50, no. 2 (April 2001): 282–304; Jeffrey L. Smith et al., "Impact of Primary Care Depression Intervention on Employment and Workplace Outcomes: Is Value Added?" *Journal of Mental Health Policy and Economics* 5 (March 2002): 43–49; Mingliang Zhang et al., "A Community Study of Depression Treatment and Employment Earnings," *Psychiatric Services* 50, no. 9 (September 1999): 1209–13.

5. *The Other America: Poverty in the United States* (1962; repr., New York: Simon and Schuster, 1997), 122.

6. Ibid., 123.

7. *The Joyless Economy: An Inquiry into Human Satisfaction and Consumer Dissatisfaction* (New York: Oxford University Press, 1976), 66.

8. Mead, *New Politics,* 66–67.

9. Today the risks need hardly be stressed in any case because they are so well known. In fact, antismoking campaigns have been so successful that the risks are actually overestimated by both smokers and nonsmokers. See Viscusi, *Smoking.*

10. Reprinted in V. C. Chappell, ed., *Ordinary Language: Essays in Philosophical Method* (Englewood Cliffs: Prentice-Hall, 1964), 58.

11. I am grateful to Elizabeth Ramey for drawing my attention to this distinction between the three forms of dysfunctionalism.

12. The label "restricted opportunity" comes from Schiller, *Economics,* 8.

13. Mai Weismantle, "Reasons People Do Not Work," *Current Population Reports,* U.S. Bureau of the Census (July 2001), 10 and 7, tables 5 and 3.

14. NPR / Kaiser / Kennedy School Poll, section II, question 7; section I, question 9; section VII, question 52.

15. As an opponent of positivism and reductionism, I will devote little space here to the quaint notion that someone's choosing not to work, with full knowledge of the consequences, *logically* proves that he or she prefers not to work. It may well be that as a matter of empirical fact human beings generally act so as to maximize the satisfaction of their preferences — indeed, I myself believe this to be the case. But to treat this as being true by definition is to stipulate an odd definition of *preference satisfaction*. Specifically, it is to equate "preference satisfaction" with "deliberate action taken with full information." By adopting this semantic approach to the empirical question of human efficiency, advocates in effect opt out of one of the oldest and most important of all debates about human behavior. Such an approach was popular during the twentieth century among so-called welfare economists. See, for instance, J. de V. Graaf, *Theoretical Welfare Economics* (1957; repr., London: Cambridge University Press, 1975), 34. But it seems to be on the wane.

16. NPR / Kaiser / Kennedy School Poll, section III, question 12; Mead, *New Politics,* 66.

17. *Losing Ground: American Social Policy 1950–1980* (New York: Basic Books, 1984). A precursor of Murray was Amos Griswold Warner, who in 1894 accused welfare of being "a source of corruption to politics, of expense to the community, and of degradation and increased pauperization to the poor. . . . The more generous public relief, the more likely the poor will prefer it to working." Quoted in David Wesell, "In Poverty Tactics, An Old Debate: Who Is at Fault?" *Wall Street Journal,* June 15, 2006, A1.

18. NPR / Kaiser / Kennedy School Poll, section II, question 9.

4. A Closer Look at the Inefficiency Argument

1. The story up through World War I is well told in George J. Stigler, "The Adoption of the Marginal Utility Theory," in *The Economist as Preacher and Other Essays* (Chicago: University of Chicago Press, 1982), 72–85. See also Emil Kauder, *A History of Marginal Utility Theory* (Princeton: Princeton University Press, 1965).

2. A common misunderstanding of the law is that it means that consumption eventually becomes counterproductive and burdensome. While that

may be true, the law itself does not deny that additional consumption continues to bring additional positive experience or relief at high levels. Instead, it asserts that the additions caused by equal increases in consumption diminish.

3. *Rationale of Judicial Evidence* (London, 1827) 5:656, quoted in Stigler, "Adoption," 74.

4. "Exposition of a New Theory on the Measurement of Risk," trans. Louise Sommer, repr. in Alfred N. Page, ed., *Utility Theory: A Book of Readings* (New York: Wiley, 1968), 199–214. See also Stigler, "Adoption," 72–85; Stigler, "The Development of Utility Theory," in *Essays in the History of Economics* (Chicago: University of Chicago Press, 1965), 66–155. Assiduous historians of economics have not found the idea of diminishing marginal utility spelled out before Bernoulli. See Kauder, *Utility Theory.* This may well be because calculus, the branch of mathematics that covers changing rates of change, had been discovered only in the seventeenth century, and only people used to thinking mathematically about changing rates of change could have conceived the law clearly. Kauder proposes this idea but rejects it on the weak grounds that Bentham *asserted* the principle in nonmathematical terms.

5. For a clear account of Weber's and Fechner's theories, see William James, *Psychology* (New York: H. Holt, 1892), 17–23. The core idea is still considered valid. See chapter 5, notes 3 and 4.

6. For example: "To see why marginal utility diminishes, think about the following two situations: In one, you've just been studying for 29 evenings. An opportunity arises to see a movie. The utility you get from that movie is the marginal utility from seeing one movie in a month. In the second situation, you've been on a movie binge. For the past 29 nights, you have not even seen an assignment. You are up to your eyeballs in movies. You are happy enough to go to a movie on yet one more night. But the thrill that you get out of that thirtieth movie in 30 days is not very large. It is the marginal utility of the thirtieth movie in a month." Michael Parkin, *Microeconomics,* 3d ed. (Reading, Mass.: Addison-Wesley, 1996), 148–49.

7. Hermann Heinrich Gossen was convinced of his own genius despite having failed in both the Prussian civil service and the insurance business. Gossen published his proposal in *Laws of Human Relations and the Rules of Human Action Derived Therefrom,* trans. Rudolph C. Blitz (Cambridge:

MIT Press, 1983). See also Stigler, "Development," 82–84. Sadly, Gossen's discovery was not influential in his lifetime. Rather, his rule was rediscovered by W. S. Jevons and several other economists in the 1870s, and it was their work that launched the so-called marginal revolution in academic economics. For more on this, see Nicholas Georgescu-Roegen, introductory essay to *Laws of Human Relations* by Gossen; R. D. Collison Black, A. W. Coats, and Craufurd D. W. Goodwin, eds., *The Marginal Revolution in Economics — Interpretation and Evaluation,* (Durham: Duke University Press, 1973). As for precursors of Gossen, the essence of his rule is repeatedly expressed in the works of Bentham; however, Bentham applies the idea only to distribution, not to allocation generally, and he makes no effort to give the idea a mathematical formulation.

8. In fact, marginalists allow as exceptions only a few types of goods — those whose benefits depend on the presence of a critical mass (sets of tires, pairs of shoes), collectibles, and addictive goods. See chapter 6 for further discussion of the critical mass, or "lumpy good," exceptions.

9. This exposition follows virtually all contemporary introductory-level economics textbooks. See, for example, Campbell R. McConnell and Stanley L. Braue, *Economics: Principles, Problems, and Policies,* 12th ed. (New York: McGraw-Hill, 1993), 405–07; Parkin, *Microeconomics,* 150–52; Paul A. Samuelson and William D. Nordhaus, *Microeconomics,* 16th ed. (New York: McGraw-Hill, 1998), 83–85. Clear historical expositions may be found in Alfred Marshall, *Principles of Economics,* 8th ed. (1890; repr., London: Macmillan, 1930), III.v.1; J. R. Hicks, *Value and Capital* (Oxford: Oxford University Press, 1939), 11–12.

10. As some readers will have noticed, the argument does not validly prove that allocators can maximize the benefit of a resource by splitting at the equal-satisfaction point unless we *also* assume that benefit is satisfaction. In other words, the argument is not valid without the added premise that well-being is felt well-being. Without this premise, the rule of equalizing satisfaction at the margin might succeed in guaranteeing that the overall *satisfaction* wrung from a resource was maximized without guaranteeing that the overall *benefit* of the resource was maximized.

But is it reasonable to adopt this added premise, the equation of benefit with felt benefit? The word *hedonism* is often used by philosophers to refer to the view that benefit is felt benefit. Antihedonists are those who differentiate between well-being and subjective well-being. Antihedonists point to cases of people who have been sublimely happy to the end of their days, but only on account of comforting illusions, and they contend that such people would have been better off, in an ultimate sense, with less utility and more truth.

Supporting this contention is the undoubted fact that many people, trying to imagine themselves in the utility versus truth dilemma, will say that this is what they would prefer — to die having had a less happy but more authentic, more "illusion-free" life. But can this preference be taken at face value? Is it not likely that such people are *trying* to imagine themselves living a life that is happy on account of comforting illusions but *failing* to imagine such a life because — making a common mistake — they equate imagining x with imagining themselves being aware of x? In effect, they are trying to imagine themselves being fooled by the comforting illusions but then smuggling themselves into the imagined scenario as all-seeing observers. Since they do not really imagine themselves being fooled after all, their distaste for that kind of life has to be discounted. On this erroneous view of imagination, see Bernard Williams, "Imagination and the Self," in *Problems of the Self: Philosophical Papers 1956–1972* (Cambridge: Cambridge University Press, 1973), 26–45.

11. *Darwin's Dangerous Idea: Evolution and the Meanings of Life* (New York: Simon and Schuster, 1995), 21.

12. See Robert S. Pindyck and Daniel L. Rubenfeld, *Microeconomics,* 5th ed. (Upper Saddle River, N.J.: Prentice Hall, 2001), 69.

5. A New Way to Rationalize the Conduct that Prolongs and Worsens Poverty

1. Herodotus, *The Histories,* trans. Aubrey de Selincourt (London: Penguin Books, 1965), bk. 1, 93–96 (paragraph break added).

2. Of course, special circumstances could make a difference. If you had just suffered six stings on your body, you *might* pay even more attention to a sting on your hand than if you had not, if you feared it might push you over the edge into a state of shock. This only shows that mechanical metaphors for attention such as dilution, squeezing down, and "jamming" are limited. It does not show that the metaphors are not generally illuminating and useful.

3. There are countless everyday examples of this phenomenon. The German

psychologist Wilhelm Wundt gives several in this passage quoted by the American psychologist William James: "The tick of the clock is a feeble stimulus for our auditory nerve, which we hear plainly when it is alone, but not when it is added to the strong stimulus of the carriage-wheels and the other noises of the day. The light of the stars is a stimulus to the eye. But if the stimulation which this light exerts be added to the strong stimulus of daylight, we feel nothing of it, although we feel it distinctly when it unites itself with the feebler stimulation of the twilight. The poundweight is a stimulus to our skin, which we feel when it joins itself to a preceding stimulation of equal strength, but which vanishes when it is combined with a stimulus a thousand times greater in amount." *Psychology,* 19. See chapter 4, note 5.

4. Modern psychophysics accepts Weber's hypothesis as "reasonably valid for a wide range of stimulus intensities, including most of our everyday experiences." Currently accepted values for "Weber fractions" include the following: for loudness, 4.8 percent; for brightness, 7.9 percent; and for heaviness, 2 percent. This means, for instance, that "2 grams must be added to a 100-gram weight, 4 grams must be added to a 200-gram weight, and 20 grams must be added to a 1000-gram weight for a difference to be detected." Harvey Richard Schiffman, *Sensation and Perception: An Integrated Approach,* 5th ed. (New York: Wiley, 2001), 38.

5. Parkin, *Microeconomics,* 148–49.

6. Relevant sentiments are expressed by Huck Finn: "At first I hated the school, but by and by I got so I could stand it. . . . So the longer I went to school the easier it got to be. I was sort of getting used to the widow's ways, too, and they warn't so raspy on me." Mark Twain, *The Adventures of Huckleberry Finn* (1884; repr., New York: Penguin Books, 2003), 24.

7. William James's famous theory of attention stressed this way of limiting phenomena to fit within the span of attention. In his phrase, attention "implies withdrawal from some things in order to deal effectively with others." *The Principles of Psychology* (Chicago: Encyclopedia Britannica, 1955), 261.

8. There are interesting differences among these cases that may be mentioned here. One difference is that with the paint scratches, the unpaid bills, the unwashed dishes, and the movies there is a logical distinction between being aware of the object and disliking it, since one could conceivably be aware of it and like it, odd as that might be in some cases. That

is what makes the affect-flipping thought experiment possible. But with the stings and patches of poison ivy one hardly knows how to distinguish between being aware of the object and detesting it. What is directly felt is not a something from which one suffers, but suffering. Yet the logical distinction in the cases of the scratches, bills, dishes, and movies between being aware of the object and having a positive or negative experience does not imply that the positive and negative experiences are processes or occurrences that could exist independently of the awareness of the object. The true relation is better represented as adverbial or modal: enjoying or detesting in these cases is more like a way of experiencing the object. We may be "miserably" aware of the scratches or the bills, and so forth. As the philosopher Gilbert Ryle notes, "It is impossible, not psychologically but logically impossible, for a person to be enjoying the music while paying no heed to it at all, or to be detesting the wind and sleet while completely absorbed in quarreling with his companion." "Pleasure," in *Dilemmas* (Cambridge: Cambridge University Press, 1954), 58–59. Holding any given affective stance, positive or negative, constant, then, we can say that the less the awareness of the object, the less the misery; and the more acute the awareness, the greater the misery. It is for this reason that having established diminishing marginal awareness of the stimuli in the car scratch type cases, we do not have to raise, as a separate question, the marginal impact of the stimulus on the perceiver's felt level of well-being. But granting that there are differences between these various kinds of afflictions, the key point is that with all of them, the mind diminishes our impression to fit within the span of attention. Thus the marginal affliction would have been much more impressive if it had been first or unique.

9. It is worth acknowledging that whether something is a pleaser or a reliever depends partly on the psychology of the consumer. Thus there are people who use what are usually considered pleasers such as jewelry to relieve their depression. In alcoholism, similarly, what is a pleaser for most people, alcohol, functions as a reliever, just as it did in the days when alcohol was used as an anesthetic, except that in alcoholism the miserable condition that is being relieved is largely the lack of the reliever itself. Conversely, there are people who get positive enjoyment from what are normally considered relievers, such as painkillers. So, strictly speaking, we should speak of something's *ordinarily* functioning as one or the other.

Yet another way in which something's being a reliever or a pleaser is relative is illustrated by the concept of health. "Health" formerly referred almost always to the absence of an evil, illness, but now it often refers to the presence of a positive good linked to strength, stamina, slenderness, and ebullience. People do not usually visit "health clubs" to relieve illness but to stimulate the production of endorphins, increase their endurance, and make themselves look better. Strictly, however, this case really reflects semantic ambiguity, not the dependence of something's being a pleaser or a reliever on the psychology of consumers. The ambiguity may be a deliberate attempt to make people consider fitness a basic good.

10. Regarding the degree of preference atypicality required to explain nonwork on the conventional theory vs. the proposed theory, see also the appendix to this chapter, "Further Exploration Through Graphical Analysis."

11. "They [African Americans in the period 1877–1954] continued to perpetuate the poverty paradigm . . . and behave as though they were prosperous, thus living in a 'shack with a Cadillac out back.'" Arthur Stovall, *The Last Remnants of Slavery* (Victoria, British Columbia: Trafford, 2005), 123. See also Cole Porter's 1919 song "That Black and White Baby of Mine," which contains the lines "She's got a black and white shack / And a new Cadillac / In a black and white design." *The Complete Lyrics of Cole Porter,* ed. Robert Kimball (New York: Knopf, 1983; New York: Da Capo Press, 1992), 66.

6. Responses to Challenges and Questions

1. I am indebted to Dr. Joan Straumanis for the idea of using "reciprocal" in this sense. The contrasting term, "polar," is used here in one of its standard senses.

2. Modern attributions of this view to Epicurus rely heavily on Cicero's account of the thought of Epicurus. Cicero lived several centuries after Epicurus, but he had access to more of his writings than we have. Among Cicero's summaries: "So Epicurus did not think that there was some intermediate state between pleasure and pain; for that state which some people think is an intermediate state, viz. the absence of all pain, is not only pleasure but it is even the greatest pleasure." *The Epicurus Reader,* trans. and ed. Brad Inwood and L. P. Gerson (Indianapolis: Hackett, 1994), 60–61.

3. *Utilitarianism* (1863), chap. 2.

4. *An Introduction to the Principles of Morals and Legislation* (1789), chap. 1, sec. 4 (emphasis added).

5. *Theory of Political Economy* 4th ed. (1871; repr., London: Macmillan, 1924), 38.

6. *Principles of Morals,* chap. 3, sec. 5.

7. *Rationale of Judicial Evidence,* 5:656.

8. In this regard, the words of Jevons are notable: "To maximize pleasure, is the problem of Economics." *Theory of Political Economy,* 37.

9. Other polar antonyms include cowardly/courageous and altruistic/self-serving.

10. *A Philosophical Enquiry Into the Origin of Our Ideas of the Sublime and Beautiful,* ed. Adam Phillips (1757; repr., Oxford: Oxford University Press, 1990), 31.

11. *Methods of Ethics,* 4th ed. (1874; repr., London: Macmillan, 1890), 124–25. For yet another argument against the Epicurean Fallacy, see Plato, *Republic,* bk. 9. Lest the reader assume that the Epicurean Fallacy is a straw man today and that our arguments against it are of only historical significance, I should point out that many of the newly popular studies of happiness by economists and policy thinkers presuppose precisely the Epicurean view I am trying to refute. For example, a "standard happiness question" asked by survey researchers at the University of Michigan's Survey Research Center runs as follows: "Taken all together, how would you say things are these days — would you say that you are very happy, pretty happy, or not too happy?" Quoted in Bruno S. Frey and Alois Stutzer, *Happiness and Economics: How the Economy and Institutions Affect Well-Being* (Princeton: Princeton University Press, 2002), 26. There is nothing inherently wrong with such a question, of course. The Epicurean Fallacy lies in the researchers' use of the question to measure the full range of perceived well-being, whereby "not too happy" comes to be equated with "unhappy."

12. Bernard M. S. van Praag and Paul Frijters, "The Measurement of Welfare and Well-Being: The Leyden Approach," in *Well-Being: The Foundations of Hedonic Psychology,* ed. Daniel Kahneman, Ed Diener, and Norbert Schwarz, 420 (New York: Russell Sage Foundation, 1999).

13. "A Biblical Response to Poverty," in *Lifting Up the Poor,* ed. Mary Jo Bane and Lawrence Mead, 68 (Washington: Brookings Institution Press, 2003).

14. See, for instance, Marianne Bertrand, Sendil Mullainathan, and Eldar Shafir, "Behavioral Economics and Marketing in Aid of Decision Making Among the Poor," *Journal of Public Policy and Marketing* 25, no. 1 (Spring 2006): 8–23.

15. While this observation is hard to support with experimental data, it is consistent with data showing that "African-Americans were generally less happy, not more so, at specific levels of income than are Caucasians." Ed Diener, Ed Sandvik, Larry Seidlitz, and Marissa Diener, "The Relationship Between Income and Subjective Well-Being: Relative or Absolute?" *Social Indicators Research* 28, no. 3 (1993): 206.

16. Richard Layard, *Happiness: Lessons from a New Science* (New York: Penguin, 2005), 48–49.

17. Daniel Kahneman and Amos Tversky, "Prospect Theory: An Analysis of Decision Under Risk," *Econometrica* 47 (2) (March 1979): 263–91. A nontechnical summary of Kahneman's and Tversky's work on this issue may be found in Matthew Rabin, "Psychology and Economics," *Journal of Economic Literature* 36 (March 1998): 11–46.

18. I am grateful to a faculty audience at a presentation I made at Yale Law School on February 15, 2005, for making me take this objection more seriously than I had before.

19. *Papers Relating to Political Economy* (London: Macmillan, 1925), 106.

20. Charles Karelis, "Distributive Justice and the Public Good," *Economics and Philosophy* 2 (1986): 113.

21. "The Measurement of Welfare," 412–33.

22. "Empirical Comparison of the Shape of the Welfare Functions," *European Economic Review* 15 (1981): 261–86.

23. "The Utility Analysis of Choices Involving Risk," *Journal of Political Economy* 56 (1948): 279–304. Note that the Friedman and Savage function actually has two inflection points. At the lowest incomes it is diminishing, then it is increasing, and then at the highest incomes it is diminishing again. They offer this as a rationalization of the facts that many low-income consumer units buy both insurance and lottery tickets and that lotteries typically have more than one prize.

24. Edwin Mansfield, *Economics: Principles, Problems, Decisions* 2d ed. (New York: W. W. Norton, 1977), 466; James P. Quirk, *Intermediate Microeconomics* (Chicago: Science Research Associates, 1976), 61–62.

25. *Principles of Economics*, 94.

26. Ibid., 92.

27. Ibid.

28. Such an equation is implicit, for instance, in Marshall's reference to "the total utility of a thing to anyone (that is that total pleasure or other benefit it yields him)." Ibid., 94.

7. Policy: *What Should We Do Differently If We Believe This?*

1. David T. Ellwood, *Poor Support: Poverty in the American Family* (New York: BasicBooks, 1988), 19.

2. New York Times poll, referenced in Schiller, *Economics,* 225.

3. For a concise account of the 1996 welfare reform and an assessment of its effects, see Schiller, *Economics,* 222–36.

4. John F. Harris and John E. Yang, "Clinton to Sign Bill Overhauling Welfare," *Washington Post,* August 1, 1996, A01. On the breadth of support for the idea of self-help, the following passage instructively tags several bases: "Some of [St. Paul's] followers imagined that they need not work, because Jesus' second coming was imminent. Paul retorts that they must earn their own living, for 'if anyone will not work, let him not eat.' That command, Michael Harrington wrote, is 'the basis of the political economy of the West.'" In this passage, a contemporary political conservative reminds us that not only Christian theology but the political left, in the person of Michael Harrington, supports self-help through work. Mead, *Lifting up the Poor,* 78. The quote from St. Paul is in 2 Thessalonians 3:10.

5. Here is how a well-known economics text presents this tenet. Given that the substitution effect encourages work and the income effect discourages work, says the text, "higher wages could lead to either a larger or smaller labor supply." But in fact, "statistical studies of this question in the United States have reached the conclusion that . . . for low-wage workers the substitution effect seems to dominate, so they work more when wages rise . . . [and] for high-wage workers the income effect seems to dominate, so they work less when wages rise." Baumol and Blinder, *Economics, Principles, and Policy* (New York: Harcourt Brace Jovanovich, 1979), 513–14.

6. Proponents of this picture point to the fact that when wages rise, more hours of labor are supplied, up to a point, after which further wage increases actually reduce hours of labor supplied. This is the so-called

backward-bending supply curve of labor. So far, so good. But the issue is, what accounts for the backward bend in the curve? The tenet that there exist two opposing pressures on motivation which change their relative strength as wages rise is not well confirmed by independent evidence, and it appears to be ad hoc. What do we know about the human mind that predicts this change in the relative strength of the two effects as income rises? Our alternative explanation of the backward-bending labor curve is that the income effect is positive at low wages and negative at high wages. This appears simpler than the conventional explanation.

7. Robert P. Stoker and Laura A. Wilson, *When Work Is Not Enough: State and Federal Policies to Assist Needy Workers* (Washington: Brookings Institution Press, 2006), 35.

8. This is consistent with a recent study of 1,075 people who applied for assistance from Wisconsin's comparatively tough welfare program in 1999. The authors state, "Like many states, Wisconsin adopted a work first approach to welfare reform. Even so, the percentage of the applicants in the study sample who were employed in any year declined steadily [through 2003] after peaking in 1999." Moreover, by 2003, the percentage employed in all four quarters was below what it had been in 1998. Mark E. Courtney and Amy Dworsky, "Those Left Behind: Enduring Challenges Facing Welfare Applicants," *Chapin Hall Issue Brief* 107 (May 2006): 5. This is also consistent with the evidence that since the welfare reform the income of the poorest 10 percent of single-mother families has fallen by more than 25 percent, adjusted for inflation. Bruce D. Meyer and James X. Sullivan, "The Well-Being of Single Mother Families After Welfare Reform," *Brookings Institution Policy Brief* 33 (August 2005): 3. Note that the authors argue that self-reported income is a poor measure of well-being, and that these families were better off by better measures.

9. On all these patterns and their rationale, see Nelson W. Aldrich, Jr., *Old Money: The Mythology of America's Upper Class,* (New York: A. A. Knopf, 1988).

10. Austin Frum conveyed this adage to me. I have not been able to make a definite attribution.

11. Quoted in Catherine Drinker Bowen, *Miracle at Philadelphia* (New York, 1986), 73.

12. See Michael Sherraden, *Assets and the Poor: A New American Welfare Policy* (Armonk: M. E. Sharpe, 1991), 146–48, 159–60.

13. See William G. Gale, J. Mark Iwry, and Peter G. Orszag, "Improving the Saver's Credit," *Brookings Institution Policy Brief* 135 (July 2004).

8. Economic Justice Reconsidered

1. *A Treatise of Human Nature* (Oxford: Oxford University Press, 1967), bk. 3, part iii, sec. 6.

2. See W. Stark, *Jeremy Bentham's Economic Writings: Critical Edition Based on His Printed Works and Unprinted Manuscripts,* vol. 1 (London: George Allen and Unwin, 1952), 116. It can only be guessed whether Bentham's personal interests, as a well-to-do Tory, figured in this judgment. Such a maneuver is to be distinguished from the search for "reflective equilibrium" recommended by John Rawls, in which one mutually adjusts one's moral assumptions and one's *moral* reactions to the policies they imply.

3. *Happiness,* 136. I will not consider here the familiar objections to this project that it requires, contrary to fact, that we can make interpersonal utility comparisons, and further assumes, again falsely, that different people's utilities from given sums cluster tightly around a mean. For good rebuttals of these objections, see Benjamin I. Page and James R. Simmons, *What Government Can Do: Dealing with Poverty and Inequality* (Chicago: University of Chicago Press, 2000), 129–31.

4. See "Income Shares by Quintile," in Schiller, *Economics,* 25, table 2.1.

5. See Victor Nee and Raymond V. Liedka, "Markets and Inequality in the Transition from State Socialism," in *Inequality, Democracy, and Economic Development,* ed. Manus I. Midlarsky, 203 (Cambridge: Cambridge University Press, 1997).

6. On the evolution of the idea of equality, see R. R. Palmer, "Equality," in *Dictionary of the History of Ideas,* vol. 2, ed. Philip P. Wiener, (New York: Scribner, 1973), 139–49.

7. Even granting that the income effect is stronger than the substitution effect here, if the goal is to maximize the amount by which this group increases its labor in response to a tax, society should consider aiming taxes not at wages but at unearned income, such as income from rents and dividends. In effect, this is taxing the income of this group in such a way as to avoid making their leisure too much cheaper. The person who is taxed in this way has a reason to work more — namely, that his income has

fallen, raising the marginal utility of earnings. But he does not have (much) reason to work less, since the tax has not directly reduced his hourly wage. But this is not a panacea because, on the negative side, this kind of tax may affect the size of the social product by discouraging saving and investing.

8. This caution should be kept in mind when interpreting the famous income maintenance or negative income tax experiments conducted by the federal government between 1968 and 1982. These have often been taken to show that transfers reduce work effort. But note that the recipients themselves reported their earnings. It may be that they so greatly underreported their earnings, to maximize their negative tax payments, that these payments simply raised them *even further above* the line of sufficiency, thus dampening their motivation for work. This would not challenge my theory, which does not deny that the incentive effects of no-strings assistance are negative above sufficiency. On these experiments, see Murray, *Losing Ground,* 147–53; Gary Burtless, "The Work Response to a Guaranteed Income: A Survey of Experimental Evidence," in *Lessons from the Income Maintenance Experiments,* ed. Alicia H. Munnell, 22–51 (Boston: Federal Reserve Bank of Boston, n.d.); Robert Moffitt, "Incentive Effects of Welfare," *Journal of Economic Literature* (March 1992): 1–62.

Index

Note: Page numbers in italics indicate graphs.

urban poverty, 14–15
utility (concept), 51, 104, 106, 130. *See also* inefficiency argument; marginalism; satisfaction

values, 46. *See also* atypical preference theories; educational persistence; work ethic
van Herwaarden, F. G., 128
van Praag, Bernard M. S., 128
Viscusi, W. Kip, 23
vocational programs, 88, 149

wages: effective wage rates and motivation to work, 136–37, 141–43, 179–80n6, 179n5 (*see also* income effect; substitution effect); minimum wage laws, 138; subsidies, 136–38, 142, 143, 144–45, 163
walk vs. bus ride example, 77–78, 84–85, 92–94, *94*, 139, 159–60
wants: vs. needs, 3–4, 109–10; utility and, 130. *See also* needs
Warner, Amos Griswold, 170n17
Weber, Ernst, 52, 70–71, 174n4
weighted sack example, 69–71
welfare system: as cause of poverty, 47–48; helping conundrum, 134–

36, 170n17; no-strings assistance, xii–xiii, 135–36, 143–44; wage subsidies, 137–38, 142, 143, 144–45, 163 (*see also* wages: subsidies); welfare reform, xii, 135–36, 137–38, 139, 180n8 (*see also* wages: subsidies)
will(power), weakness of, 36–38
Wisconsin welfare program, 180n8
work ethic, 46, 115. *See also* nonwork; working for pay
workaholism, 79–80
working for pay: alcohol abuse and, 22; career-specific training, 88, 149; effective wage rates and motivation to work, 136–37, 141–43, 179–80n6, 179n5 (*see also* income effect; substitution effect); and the increasing marginal utility hypothesis, 82–83; increasing marginal utility hypothesis and, 95–99, *96*, *97*; part-time/low-wage jobs as poverty cause, 23; policies to encourage, 133–47, 161–62; restricted opportunities theory and, 42–44; U.S. statistics, 15–17, 43. *See also* employment; nonwork
Wundt, Wilhelm, 174n3